M

Moods

Of times and thoughts of love…

By

James Love

A Soldier & A Poet

There is no one individual that I could dedicate these pieces of poetry to. The list is far too long. There would be those who would think that the words I have written are solely about them. There are those who may never see the book at all and will never know. I hope that they might resonate with some and bring a smile.

To all the women who have passed through my life. The good ones, the bad ones, the beauties and the not so beauteous. All who have in some way made a lasting impression on me. Some not so much so, but possibly contributed to the man I am now.

My granddaughter Raynah-Mae who is on the front cover of this book. The light of my life.

To Dream...

A lifetime of memories
Some lost...
Some, never to be forgotten!
Of places, things and people.
Which have made an impact.
Upon my life.
And now...
With fresh and new.
To fill the void!
A scent, a smile, a pair...

Of blue eyes.

CONTENTS

1) My Life, Was Written

In a book, that is, on a table,
found.
In that great Hall…
Named
Valhalla…
Written,
with a thousand-year-old ink.
Which faded, from the page.
Before my name,
Even dried.
We're Family…
I used to think that death,
Mayhap was a punishment.
The thirst of life quenched…
Before I'd drank my fill!
Perhaps I've got it wrong?
Life may be the punishment!
For with death,
There is no further pain…

After all.

2) *Sybaritic, but I Promised Not to Tell*

A sensuous pleasure… Perhaps if,
You were to catch me… if,
I'm smiling.
Or even, if… I'm blue!
Perhaps,
you want to share, a… tomorrow.
Or merely...
Just a moment… of my time.
For, right here, for, right now.
And if I got a kiss...
I promise

not to... tell.

3) I Whispered As

The darkness called.
And its cries, echoed... in the night.
I'm cold
No rest, for me.
The rhythmic beating, of... my heart
Is stilled.
There's a, chill...
Upon, my soul.
It's a long time, since... I felt,
the wet sand, beneath...
bare feet.
Or a lover's subtle breath
Upon
My lips.
There's a sadness in my eyes.
That's killed, the spark.
Life, withers...
For

Death, called out my name.

4) All the Colours of a Rainbow?

The scent of your love.
If I could, just transcend...
Those moments... to a colour.
It might be...
The colour, of your eyes.
Of a morning.
Or perhaps...
The colour, of your lips.
Of a moonlit evening.
Or
The colour of... your blushes.
In moments of wanton... passion.
Which lingered like a rainbow.
But is all gone now!
Causing my eye to jade.
I no longer know the scent!
Am therefore, am rendered... .
colour blind.
As while I forlornly search,
for that lover's... litany.
And all the while I do...
My current colour, is...

A paler shade of Blue.

5) *Could You Hear That...*

A sound… so fine.
While I slept…
Winds howled,
As waves, smashed!
Upon, many different shores.
And around the world…
Guns roared, and people died.
But above it all…
Was it was only I
Who, heard…
That

A butterfly, was crying?

6) I Dream To

Life's full of dreams, where...
Childish dreams,
are meant to fade and die.
Impossible dreams,
are meant, to fail...
because we didn't try.
Our worst thought dreams...
Turn into nightmares!
Because love got in the way?
Or we never shared!
Or we cared...
Too

Much.

7) I'll Take It

It's your smile.
I truly, fell in love with!
Its wickedness, reflected…
In your eyes.
A pixie-like voice,
That could command.
Whilst, full of passion.
Didst…
Melt, a stony heart.
And caused, a tear… to dwell.
For all my life,
A regret, for all time.
A memory, of love.
To take…

To my grave.

8) *Hold Me as I Sleep, and Kiss Me*

Just...
Make, sweet love... To me.
Teach me, to... dance!
Meet me... there.
Amongst, the stars!
Take my hand, and... Steal my heart.
I, now have the keys... to,
the asylum.
And caused, a tear... to dwell.
So come, and set me free.
Just, share with me, for the moment.
Don't try to understand me.
Don't look too deep.
You won't like... what you see.
Keep the colours loud, and keep them bright.
Drown, reality,
in fizzy wine and froth.
All, I'm asking... of you,
Is...
Tell me, that you love me.
And, be there,
In the morning

When I awake.

9) I Kissed, a Myriad, of... Light

It's just…
How, to kill a wish!
Sometimes a wish, is so obscure.
It lays beyond, the realms, of fantasy.
So we no longer dream, of it… encore.
And once the spirit of love's verse is, lost…
I searched, within a memory.
For a dream.
And saw that girl, from the squat…
that played, the guitar,
so well.
Another… The barmaid…
Not forgetting the redhead, that shaved.
And I only knew...
the true colour of her hair,
becausee told me.
Long forgotten memories
That happened before, an epic… journey
I once made in life.
And could I ever forget, that…
Summer

in Bexley Heath?

10) The Fabric of Our Being, Is...

A letter to Althea?
When I was in jail.
I wrote one similar, from the Traz.
But not four walls...
For one was full of bars.
I washed my clothes, in a sink.
I dried them, hanging
From, my windows...
And they never smelled, more sweeter!
Nor, were any cleaner, than
A free man's

Clothes.

11) Did You Ever

Kiss, a...
Wisp?
Or taste an exotic drink, they don't make, no more... ?
Or wish, there was more to life
Than just, foolish whims?
Sombre, are my thoughts.
While my memories, are... murky, black.
You were, that... tree,
full of, forbidden... fruit!
That was, so lush, once plucked.
I kept going back, for more.
Sweet, was the taste, of sin.
And so I ask...
Why?
And would I
Ever

Know... ?

12) There Could Never Be...

Whence on rain-painted streets.
Under a waning moon and falling stars.
My life and dreams were... Shared.
Remembering,
the sparkle in your eyes.
The mischief, in your laugh,
and star shine... From your smile.
All, t'while... I'm missing,
the warmth, of your lips on...
Winter nights.
And how you held me tight.
Tis no other's heartbeat, I wish to hear.
I long to pass each majik moment, like enchanted
lovers, caught in a pleach.
As I could never, share again...
With

... anyone but you!

13) 470 Nanometres, It's Just

If you know her...
Could you, pass this along, from me?
The nights, have grown darker, and... lonelier,
now, that you have gone.
I no longer see, a sparkle, in...
blue eyes.
With which, the twinkling, of the night's stars
I did, once... compare.
The sky, it seems, has now, lost its lustre.
While, I have lost.
My
Lovely eyes...
Of

Blue.

14) Whisper...

My name.
Like, I once, whispered… yours.
In the dark, of the night,
while, holding… you close.
Or, when we were apart.
Or when, I felt the want, of your love.
I'll forever whisper your name.
When,
an Angel's feather, touches, my heart.
When I'm melancholy, and feeling lonely.
When I think, I can smell,
Your… perfume.
Or I thought I heard your voice, upon the wind.
Your voice is embedded, in my soul.
So just…
Whisper

My name…

15) I No Longer Cast A Pebble, For

I heard the sadness, in your voice.
That showed me, the colour, of...
your soul.
And it matched, the purity...
of your eyes.
Oft, I hear, their... silent call.
And wonder...
Should I respond
Or just wait, my turn... ?
While in my eyes... there's
A deadness, to match
The colour, of their shrouds.
There's a darkness, that...
Fills my heart.
To catch
Those

ripples on the pond.

16) Today It's

Rain...
It rained.
And rained.
And rained.
And it's still

Raining.

17) Send Me

Flowers,
For... I love
Their vibrant colours, and
Their, sweet, scent.
For, I miss my love,
and, the colours...
She didst bring!
And just like her, they'll not long, last.
But, a brief beauty...
Full of life, before they wilt,
and die
But, while they're here
They'll, be... mine!
My tears, are real.
But my dreams, are made... of, smoke!
Which have dissipated, in the wind.
Like a fallen rainbow.
Like the discarded petals.
Of, my now...
Dead

Flowers.

18) I Once Tasted...

Freedom, long ago.
And…
It was sweet, and like, no… other.
'Cept, perhaps, that… of love.
Though…
Now not for me… I'll no longer seek that spice
of life.
It brings no joy.
For it left bitter, splenetic reminder.
A taint, that spoiled fruit, doth sometimes have.
That permeates a soul.
And…
Kills

A sweet taste.

19) And All I Know Is

In clear skies
Or when the heavens are opaque
Your beauty shines like no other.
You have that gift of life
A fragility, an honesty, a truth!
And I've heard all your words.
I'm blind, to your song.
Your Majik, killed my reason.
Your beauty, stole my life.
While death, ever pursues me.
I clutch a slender thread,
That holds a tangible, dream.
And, I'm like a little boy again.
I want to hold you close,
Smell the seasons, on the wind.
Touch a faerie… kiss
A, waif…
Live in the shadow,
Of

Your love.

20) Had I'd Not... Been Given The

The chance… If only.
To share a thousand sunrises.
And if given?
I'd have shared them all, with you.
And if, I dreamed, a dream.
I'd have dreamed, a dream, of you.
Only if
I'd had a brief tangere in life.
It…
Would only

taste, of you.

21) Once...

My tears were sweet,
and
Full of joy.
I'd watch the stars.
While waiting, for the moon.
As smoke drifted off.
Carried by the wind.
Liccian
Mayhap, just broken.
Crumbling dreams...
Like, falling autumn leaves.
Cast upon, an empathetic stream.
That now eddy, in a corner.
 Deep within my mind.
A mistake...
That's come to haunt me.
Of a love I've lost.
All that while... for
Once

You played my song.

22) Why

Why, is nothing ever simple with you?
Why, does it always bring me tears?
Why, is nothing ever simple with you?
Why... Just, Why?

23) Wretched, We Languish In

As emotion, can truly blind us.
For we fail to see, what others do!
And fail, to recognise, the pain
That our own suffering, causes
To those, around us…
And so, we all suffer, together.
Miserably
Alone…
And,
in

Silence.

24) Not All Dreams Happen In

Our lifetime, though once…
Long ago.
In a temple, of the Mayans.
Upon, a… crumbling wall.
They foretold my fate.
Before skies, were even, blue.
They went, and told it… all!
Of how I met, and, lost... a love.
Of dragons, and fiery birds.
A tale, synonymous… with you.
And then they wrote it, a book.
Where poets, spread the tale.
Of a love, beyond… one man's dreams.
And how it was, borne to fail.
Now I'm waiting for, that Airborne… Moon.
That's coming, before… this dawn.
When the stars shine.
And heaven, reflects… of death.
And the moon glows… blood red!
Where only soldiers stand on guard…
and, stare.
While lonely lovers lie… alone,
in

bed.

25) You May, Not Have Been

Perfect.
But you were, at least… my,
Imperfection!
And what, 'twas not, to love?
How, can I let you go…
When I don't know, where…
You've gone?
So
Let me… go.
If, you've done with me now.
Unchain, my heart, and
Set me free!
I've watched, you as you sleep.
I've seen, the sadness… in your eyes.
I kissed your lips, 'n' tasted, all… your lies.
While all I ever dreamed
Was

True love…

26) When Life's...

Wine, has lost, its… sweetness.
When, a jejune horse, appears.
As it comes, upon the dawn.
I'll be in that group of four.
My last chance, at love… Then.
For,
I'd rather smell, a rose's scent
Than that, of death, or fear.
And if you should you share, a kiss..
That'd melt, a dragon's heart.
Perhaps one last time.
Before, you stretch… your wings.
Before, a feather… falls.
And if not…
Take me now
For
My heart is lost.
My life

no longer a pleasure.

For Claire Baker because she asked.

27) I've Known In My …

Times… of many things.
A dream… a knowledge.
I've known… beautiful women.
I know, beautiful… people.
Once I knew happiness.
Now
I know, the loneliness… of
Being, in a crowd.
Perhaps, sadness, feeds my words
That help, to fill a page.
But, not enough, to fill…
The book,
of

life.

28) Bring On The…

Beige heels,
on slender legs.
Little brown boots,
that click…
when you walk.
That air, of haughtiness
That sets, you apart.
My heart
Is in your hands.
Remembering… your laugh!
For your smile, is engrained.
Forever, what, that was you…
For me, still remains.
Each night
I kiss, a forgotten dream.
While each waking moment,
I dance, within a happy tune.
As your eyes flash with fire.
My heart is full…
Of

Chill… a lost desire.

29) Who Will Sing...

Who, knows my song?
When, the lady sings...
She gives me, the blues.
For...
She's... "the song",
that lifts my heart.
The one,
That... makes me cry.
Some say...
You've been, a bitch... to me.
But, I'm not... one.
And I guess that's why.
Although, you broke my heart
I'm still in love with you!
And... I'm
Waiting... for your return.
For, until, you do
My life, is full... of emptiness.
There's, no echo...
Of

My song.

30) For Those…

That I'd once, met,
I never said, I didn't… love you.
I just, never, said…
I did.
In the sweetness, of night.
There's a bitterness, left unsaid.
Of…
my love… and all
Of those
who've gone.

31) What Do You See?

When you close your eyes. Is it me?
Where do you go?
Are you with me?
Or a land far away,
in brutal night heat
where your tears
and your sweat become one,
and you pray for the light!
For the day!
For the sun!
And your heartbeat melts into the night.
What do you see when you wake?

Is it me?

32) Why...

Why,
Do your fingers tremble?
Is that a tremor,
In your voice?
Why do,
You quiver...

So?

33) Anterior, a Hooded Frenulum of

You said your daddy taught you
But I never heard you play
And now I guess I never will.
Or perhaps it was just another lie.
Who knows where love's melody
Takes us all...
Who hears its music
We all, have to have, a reason, to be.
Simple gestures...
A smile, or... to hold a hand.
To flick, a fleck, that's just not there!
A bond, an empathy.
That's much, much more
Than just

mere love, how I miss it so.

34) Love You Baby…

So… What's, there not to love?
Everyone's wanting miracles.
And I'm waiting, for the call.
But I'm on the downward spiral.
Just trying, to please, them all!
So… what's not to love,
And, would you ever say?
My flowers have all wilted.
The petals, are all gone.
A memory, of a moment,
Through the scent, still lingers on.
So… what's not to love?
And, I miss you every day.
Sunlight filters through the glass.
From, a creeping dawn, finding…
A rumpled bed!
And, you've gone.
Love you baby… and

So… What's not to love?

35) Missing You ...

Is more, than just, an emotion!
It's tearing, my heart... in two.
I have never felt, the passion,
That you, make me do.
I just want to...
wrap my arms, around you.
Smell, the essence... in your hair,
Kiss your tender lips,
Smell... beautiful,

again.

36) I'll Sleep... That

I'll remember you.
Whilst, I sleep.
Hoping... that.
You'll, remember me.
As I, sleep... that,

Eternal sleep.

37) Left…

I cry,
for no other reason
Than just… saying,
your name.
It cuts, my breath
When, you're not… there,
…and I hear no answer.
Or when I reach out,
To touch… Empty air.
I miss you, so, so… much!
Sometimes,
I think… my life's,
Just… about

Over.

38) Bad Bits And…

Who knows…
Perhaps, this is all,
A dream.
And I should,
Only remember,
The…

Good bits.

39) Once Upon...

My tears, hold questions
That have, no answers.
And as such,
I am lost...
Within, that myriad.
For all,

Time.

40) One Time...

A simple touch.
From...
One.
I miss... so
Much.
Is all,
I long for...

Erstwhile.

41) Over And…

Come meet me…
In that moment,
before the dawn.
When death…
treats all men equal.
A time… to check in,
Before checking…

Out!

42) Life…

In the morning of my youth.
When I laughed, at life's dreams.
I never saw, beyond the sunset.
And never,
searched for the dawn.

I never learned.

43) The Honourable Woman... That's

I'm hiding, behind my words.
And if… it takes a millennia
Before, you say.
I'll still be here… waiting!
Like I do… every single day.
I want to crush, your fears.
Hold you tight…
and wipe away, your tears.
Hear you sigh, stop you…
if you cry.
I just wanna be,
Somewhere… close to you.
So I can smell... your beautiful.
And taste… a wonderful,
To be a part, of life.
That includes…

You.

44) For You... My Own

I'd take that leap, for...
You, are the sunshine
That warms my day.
Your words, comfort me,
And, make my heart sing.
I live, to hear your voice!
Hold you close,
and touch, your smile.
I know, no other...
You are, my soulmate!
My own...

True lover.

45) True Love... No

I know...
It'd be, safe to say... that
I have a fascination with you!
But, that'd be a lie.
For, I'm really...
Totally...

infatuated, with you!

46) I Know ...

I know, I said.
I haven't said.
For a while…
But you told me,
That I say it, every day!
And I know, I do.
For… It's true

I miss you.

47) You're My Own Alice…

The teapot's full of gin
And the Mad Hatter's dancing…
With Sailor Jerry!!!
While me…
I'm chasing, the white rabbit!
But he's too… far ahead.
I'm spiralling,
out of control…
And my heart's ready…
to burst.
I'd like, to sing a song.
But,
I don't know the words.
For,
it's just a tune,

in my head.

48) I Met You... Once.

500 years, before.
For it takes that long, to nurture.
Of life, of soulmates
And true love, must be sure…
Ticking, always, ticking…
That, invisible clock, that measures… emotion.
If a face, could launch, a thousand ships!
Could not, that same love,
But… conquer, a lost lover's heart?
I'll have chance of dying… in,
Bed

But I'd be dying alone!

49) My Flower…

My love...
Has bruised your lips.
Though tender, was my touch.
I quenched my thirst, amidst...
A roaring, in my ears.
And I was lost, upon...
A wave of lust.

How sweet you taste.

50) *Sometimes I Need Someone...*

Sometimes...
we all need, someone.
To smile at us... smile, with us.
Make us laugh,
and we'd hear their laugh too.
To hold a hand,
To give a hug, or just a kiss!
Someone to talk to,
someone to listen...
Someone to say,
I love you.
Someone one to tell...
That you miss them
so can tell them that...
That, you love them,
And to just hope,
That they miss you
And that they love you

Too.

51) We're Not Perfect

I think that's why…
We're all chasing rainbows.
Why we all search the sky.
At times… we
Try to catch moon beams,
While we reach for the stars.
A tentative stab at reality.
While our dreams…
Melt around us.
Expectations swirling,
Down a sink.
Sometimes…

Angels do… Crash and burn too.

52) Once

That
Briefly I'd, had, a moment
Of pure happiness… nay
Total Wonderment.
And it was all…

Just, for me!

53) All I Have

I'd got a feather…
From a Phoenix!
Which healed, my ills.
Now I'm laughing…
While drinking, with the gods.
I'm at the tables, in Valhalla.
For, there's only them... that see.
That sharing love
with a mystic being.
Of how lonely... one can be.
How a brightly coloured
feather,
Cured my all.
And it was all...
I had,

of she.

54) Haiku 7

When the moon is full,
And your heart is empty.
I'll think of you.

55) You Rock

I'm dancing…
with German, Kriegsmarine!
While Jerry's, chopping ice…
The python's sniffing coke!
The nights, got rather wild.
And now we're going for broke.
The sailors on the bottle,
The band's in full swing.
The music's kind of haunting
It's wonder…
we're still afloat.
The place is really trashed.
But…
I've just had a happy thought
Cause it's…
Not

My boat.

56) We Share A Bond, Anima Mundi

If you've ever heard,
the sound,
From a babbling brook,
Then you've heard, her laugh.
And, if you've ever felt.
The, warmth of the wind,
After a summer's downpour,
Then you know, her touch.
If you've looked in a new-born's eyes,
You'll understand, the softness,
Of her soul.
I'll walk this world alone.
Until my time is come.
And I'll never, find… another.
For, she

Is the one.

57) I'll Just Tell You...

You make me... live,
So I can view the morrow.
To see, the rising...
Of... the morning's sun.
You're the reason,
I see each sunset...
Feel the wind, and hear the rain.
You're my raison d'être!
And I can't wait, to see
You...

Again.

58) Lukewarm, As Cold As

When the hot tears of passion...
Met the cold tears of remorse.
It cleansed... my soul.
Warmed my heart...
Set me, a target,
A new life's goal!
Be it said,
Tears without passion...
Are like a Jura,
Without...

Ice!

59) My Feelings For

Infinity… an,
unmeasurable, distance.
Love… an,
unfathomable, feeling.
All of which,
I have, for…

You.

60) Without…

Sadness,
has tinged…
my life.
And I've felt…
your pain.
I move… within,
a salient world.
Where,
I've seen a life,
I wished, I'd had.
And I'd, wished…
That, I'd, had it,
With…

You.

61) Phoenix Or...

Ominous, is…
an unwritten sound.
Where mortality,
Irrespective… what you say,
Is a bet, I once had.
I think of you, every single day.
For, if tonight, I go to sleep…
And, never see…
the morrow's dawn!
I'll forever, see your face.
And I know no other,
For – you, are my

Fay.

62) It's You

I've seen.
Where water flows,
As clear, as crystal.
And summer, fills…
The sky.
I'll say your name.
That on fair wind,
You'll hear…
Amidst,
that downpour's thrall.
The pitter patter
of my heart.
Saying… I miss you
as it calls.
For truly, it's you…

I love.

63) Tranquillity

No fear of dying.
We are… immortals!
Our death's, already, begun.
Soldiers of St Michael…
Airborne, everyone!
No love, to share.
No one, to care.
Just war, beer…

and death!

64) Never Would I…

Cause you tears.
I, could cry…
Forever.
For, the regrets…
That I, have had.
But… I'll never regret.
Loving you!
Nor make you cry…

because of it.

65) More Than Just Memories It's

I danced within the moonlight.
While…
My song was sung,
before the dawn!
I can say…
No more.
Sometimes, there's a certain fragrance,
Which is attributed to places...
Or persons… or moments,
in time!
A persona you can't forget.
And I can't help saying,
I miss you…
40 times a day.
Nor would I ever want to
It's a memory... more than,
Just

Nostalgia.

66) Rain Stopped

Because…
You, bring me…
sunshine!
When you come and stay.
You warm… my heart
On wintry… days.
While teardrops fall…
Like fresh, raindrops.
They'll leave no trace,
…on a summer's day.
For love's…
Just an emotion!
At which we

Play.

67) Echoes and Strange...

From the ashes.
I sing, your name.
From...within, my poetry.
All about...
My dreams, for you!
My words, oft telling them...
Of... your beauty!
Of my... loves lost.
Of blue eyes...
Clear skies.
Lust... 'n'...
Lovers'

Cries.

68) I Thought I Heard You

We share a bond,
Hanging…
within a chain.
That we both wear…
Around our neck.
While, Odin's sent, fair maid.
Bellerophon, has loaned his steed.
And winged brothers,
ever watch…
that rainbowed bridge.
Should we

call.

69) I Love It All Especially…

No time, to kill…
For there's a tiger, in the cage.
I'm going where…
Emotions, take me.
Where mere… moods
Are like, faerie dust…
Amidst, the forest floor.
As spider webs… shiver.
And sunlight burns…
the morning dew.
Babies feed, from mothers' milk.
All the while, I'm thinking of you.
I'm travelling, through time.
For, we never know…
what, the morrow brings.
That's why,
we hold… the moment.
Untenable dreams… are…
what it seems.
And not what, reality…
holds for us.
But, still… we chase that dream.
Hold me tight… lest I vanish, within…

Your dream this night.

70) Empathy…

I'm overdosing, on emotion.
And it's leaking, from my ears.
And I just don't know…
And I really, can't say… why.
My salt's, all thrown…
My heart's set, on speed dial!
And I've got sumo…

on the brain.

71) Destined Forever To Be

Celebrating, a dream.
That's, vanished…
in a haze, of alcohol!
Washed, away…
by the wind, and rain.
Now left,
Standing, alone!
In a puddle, of loneliness.
Once, again…
I'm

On my own.

72) My Canvas Is Blank, It's Still

I live beyond, that…
Which is the pale.
For I know,
no need,
to lie!
My life's a book,
With scattered crayons…
on the floor of life.
Therein… my pages,
Still… unread.
Of which, the pictures…
All remain,

uncoloured.

73) We'll Meet Again...

Weep, my tears... and,
Share... my misery.
None can know.
'Cept those... that's been!
And in the morning,
My pain, will end.
Until...

Next year.

74) Say My Name, and Remember

But...
Don't cry for me.
Don't, waste your tears.
If you whisper... my name,
I'll hear it, in your dreams.
There I'll share... a moment,
While... you sleep.
Where I'll linger, until...
the memory, fades.
And... you no longer,
See... my,

My face...

75) Let's Get Back

It may not, be an end.
For all we know,
It may just be…
A step, back in time!
To happier days,
Beneath, a friendly sun.
Where, we can all gather…

Together.

76) Never Could Say Either…

Apparently, we all know each other's moods.
We have a bond that makes it so.
We chat, on here, we chat,
in the pubs… at social get-togethers.
We chat, with partners, and with friends.
All benign, lost within each, other's thoughts.
A complexity, none can know.
Set by a thought. A smell, a memory.
Perhaps a setback.
Who knows for it is buried deep.
And a question before I sleep.

No… nor goodbye?

77) Je T'aime

Not for why
But for
Who

Forever & Always.

78) I Howled...

Upon the wind
I smelled your scent.
A memory
Heaven sent,
An empty dream.
Of who I knew...
And what I'd seen.
Of loves lost,
And
Beauty steeped,

In pain.

79) Empty Tears...

Just what I have,
From missing you.
I'm no longer...
Chasing a dream!
I'm trying, to catch...
A memory,

Before it disappears.

80) No

I saw a dream,
Within your eyes,
That broke my heart.

Illusions.

81) I Remember When

Dragonflies…
In the noonday sun.
Chasing ripples…
On a pond.
Where love's just,
An illusion.
Destiny's child… I know,
Must have smiled, when fate…
Took the day off.
And…

I met you!

82) One Last Dance…

I sit within…
a nostalgic moment.
Where dreams,
…and consequence… mingle.
Where truth is a virtue,
And…
Glib lies flourish.
Amidst the ruins…
Of my life.
It's a long time,
Since I smelt beautiful…
And I've paid the piper,

For the privilege.

83) If You Search Deep Enough

There's a song in my heart,
Which is fed,
from the music in my soul.
…A haunting melody,
that only I… can hear.
Though its lyrics… are endless,
It's the warrior's overture!
And if I play it now, for you,
Could you hear it.?
Amongst a cacophony of the dying.

It's where… we will find ourselves.

84) I Had... A

Be careful… lest you get,
The taste.
I'm lost… within your arms.
When I've got,
The taste.
Like a soulful drink.
To take one sup…
Is not enough.
So I return to, my lover's cup.
To quench my thirst,
Slate my fill.
Drink deep, taste the Chill.
Upon my lips you linger
For they are full.
For… I've had a…

Taste!

85) No Need of Names for...

Off to bed,
And on to dreams.
Of wishes and regrets!
And a chance to taste...
One more time,
those sweet lips!
Whilst I sleep.

You know who you are...

86) I See

Your plumage... fills my world with light.
Though my eyes, are dimmed with age.
My thoughts of love...
Which come from the heart... are truly,
Filled with majik!
Flowing through, my very being,
Are words that torch my soul.
For mere words can never show
Of how I feel... for, you!
A bird of paradise.
My princess...
Ryujin's own

φοίνιξ

87) I'm Out of Step, I'm Out... Of

Tears…
All turned,
To dust.
Dreams…
Swallowed,
By the mists, of

time.

88) Babylon

If I shed.
A thousand tears...
To live.
A thousand years.
Would you share,
A few tears...
With me?

Perhaps...

89) Early Morning Traveller... Are

I've been on my own now,
For quite, some time.
It's been,
So… so… long.
That I've forgotten…
the sound of your voice,
or your face…
as you smiled!
I've forgotten the reason…
I cry…!
It's all down…
…to

You…

90) I'd Like to Be Adventurous

It would seem,
There are new rivers,
For me…
To drift on.
Green foothills to walk.
With distant, mountains to cross!
Bringing, fresh vistas to view.
Should I, reverse,
The sands, of time…
Or, choose to take.
A different path…

With you.

91) Looking

I hope…
soulmates,
meet… in heaven,
I really do.
For I've spent,
an eternity.
Just looking…

For you.

92) What I Loved Most Was

The fresh fragrance of your scent,
The pale softness of your hair.
The goose bumps on your arms,
As we accidentally touched.
A sparkle in your eye.
That hinted promise, of so much!
While silent lips,
fed an aching heart.
Indelibly etched upon...
A love-fevered brain.
Endlessly and for...

The Moment.

93) In My Life's Dreams

In a world beyond?
Serendipity.
Where perfection,
Rules the realm.
A love, so true.
It burned my brain,
And stopped, my heart.
No one knows…
For none were there,
And so, none, have seen!
My eyes had drowned,
Amidst the tears,
I had shed, for you.
But, when I see your smile,
My heart, just stops.
And I wonder… at my luck.
Musing… as, to how?
I'd missed you, long before.
I wish…
I wish, I wish, I wish…
And I did!
And…

I got you.

94) I Live It... All

I do it all.
And perhaps,
One day... "my words"...
will be loved!
And mayhap shared...
when I am no more.
And till then... I'll live
the poet's life!
Full of lost moments,
Loneliness
and despair.
I've lost my love,
and I guess I'll die...

alone?

95) Yesterday…

And now.
I'm sad…
not, being with you.
While deep,
in the darkest, reaches…
of my heart.
A tiny spark.
Fed… by a memory,
locked within my brain.
Causes a warmth,
to fill… my being.
My only, raison d'être.
As only time stands still.
Forever & Always…
Till we meet,

Once more.

96) For Once, I...

The moon was full,
But not my heart.
And sadness, filled the skies.
Darkness, hid the sorrow.
That only lovers, know!
While moonbeams, mocked.
The night dragged on.
As my, star...

failed to shine.

97) *Within My Dreams... I*

You got me to breathe again.
You even…
taught me dance!
You coloured, my world…
with true romance.
The tears,
that I now weep,
Are for the shadows, you've cast…
Across my heart.
To once again,
taste your fragrance.
Sweet…
Upon my lips.
Hold you close,
To…

Feel that chill…

98) I Share The

Pain.
Though, I know I be
A distant love,
I know your face... for it
Mirrors your heart.
For what I cannot see.
While, I empathise... I also
mourn with you.
As I listen.
Your voice...
Such a sweet Spirit,
Now echoes... Only,

Sadness.

99) I Cry For You, While... We're

It seems, that tears…
Are full of snowflakes!
Of the kind, that melts a heart.
Or chills the soul…
When lovers, are

Apart.

100) Up, Up and…

I can't bring you…
Sunshine!
No…
Not, this late, in the day.
Nor, can I bring you...
Moonbeams.
So… to help,
Light your way.
That creeping sadness
Has shown, within your eyes,
For the clouds, behind you heart.
Have chased… all the rainbows

away!

101) Of Us...

I remember...
crystal-clear waters.
Summers... that were so hot...
You couldn't breathe.
Winters... so cold,
the rain froze!
But most of all,
I'll remember you.
Your laugh, your smile.
The colour... of your eyes.
Your scent, your tears,
The sum... of all your fears.
Lost, in the myriads...
Of time and mist.

I'll Always Remember You.

102) If I'd Dance... Rainbows Then

And who could see…?
Who, would herald the morrow?
Lay, testament… Of today!
Of what, future winds,
may bring.
Of hollow pipes, and music.
Wherein.. no one sings!
Nor violins,

would ever play.

103) Fate or Miss…

Who knows, what the morrow brings.
What pain, still lays, within.
Hidden behind dead eyes.
I've drank, deep… from that well.
Tasted, its sweet contents.
Saw… its dark, desire.
Its secret, want,
For fame, or…

Fortune?

104) Not All Boys Are Made

Look into my eyes,
And…
Read my heart.
See my sorrow,
Which…
Lays within.

Of ceiling wax, and balls of string.

105) Not Slings, Nor Arrows Nor

Does that breath, of air,
Which whispers, 'pon
A summer's breeze,
Bring solace...
For a lonely heart?
Or is it an icy chill,
That kills, love's flame?
That'd cause you to,
Kiss

A poisoned chalice?

106) Your Love Has Burned

There's a firestorm,
in my brain.
That's fuelled…
by the vodka,
I have drunk.
And it's destroyed…
a sensible part,
of my body.
It's helped to break…

My heart.

107) Delightful... No

For me, to sum up… my love,
In only, one word.
Would be… to say,
You're…

Delicious!

108) I Have No Understanding... Of

I fell in love.
And I fell in love, with you.
And I never want, to share... my love.
With anyone, else… but you!

The rules of emotion.

109) It's Life

Too stupid, to understand.
To drunk, to comprehend.
Too inept, in love to know.

And it's my life.

110) My Love Is…

I meld with nature.
I melt, into the dark.
I merge… with the planet.
I become as one…
And my pain?
Is…
Like my love,

Infinite.

111) *Because You're Not Home I'm*

…waking up alone.
And it don't feel right.
It's cause… you're not there!
My heart, misses… a beat,
And my throat is dry… while
you've filled up my head.
But, not my bed…!
I'm lying here… all… alone.
It's really… not… fair!
But if I say… I want you…
You think…
I'm just trying to haunt you…!
No it's really… just… not… fair!
I just don't want to…
keep on,

Waking up, all alone…!

112) Ah

The sweetest, smelling, thing,
I know of, has perhaps now, faded…
From my life… forever,
And…

I miss her terribly!!!

113) Frosty Nights, Rainy Days And

All I have are words!
Which seldom, if ever…
bring me comfort.
More often, a mere reminder, of sad times.
Or of happy times, I've now lost!
And thus, so are also now, part of my,
Sad times.
Even on…

Sunny afternoons.

114) *Woe*

Once again.
An epic fail.
Mere words…
what, would I know?
Of the emotion
That they could conjure up.
More like, I am a novelty…
A hapless jester!
A fool, lost… and out of,
His depth… is who… ?

Is me!

115) I Could Smell

And so I smiled…
Feeling the planet,
As I walked.
Beneath my feet.
For,
It felt… good, and…
I bonded with it, there and then.
Under a dark sky.
Which showered me…
Like a snow storm.
with,

…elder blossom petals.

116) My Life's Song, Is Without

There's a rhythm…
being played, within my heart.
Which is causing me… pain.
But in another light,
causes me also, to rejoice!
And in turn is, buried deep.
Just a silent… something.
Kindling… a little flame.
That lights my life, and…
makes me happy.
But why?
For…
I just don't know,
All the… melody, nor the…

words.

117) Flowers...

Are, like doors.
One closes, while another...
Opens!
Petals, wilt and die.
While fresh buds...

Blossom.

118) I Have an Image

I see once again,
you've scrubbed up well!
With your rosy cheeks,
and alabaster skin.
Soft... as freshly fallen snow.
All the while you're smelling,
like the frozen tundra's flowers.
Their long-lost scent,
swept along, by icy blasts...
from a forgotten wind.
Frozen in time,
Like your picture...

Frozen in my mind.

119) In The Night... It

Of cotton tails, and vivid fauna.
Colours beyond the pale!
And in the morn, when you awake.
The fairies' dust…

Has cleansed your dreams.

120) I'm Clever With My Words

No lovey-dovey, shit.
I miss you… simples,
Isn't it?

No shit babe!

121) Once Again… Apparently

I'll make the best of it.
After all...
I'm getting back,
into the swing... of,
solitude.
No one's with me,
So who's to tell me...

I've fucked up?

122) Vodka…

We don't always get what we want in life.
Or
So
They say…
It's all about?
What you mean to me.
How I feel about you,
And how we feel about each other.
So you just gotta get up and make your play.
Don't cha worry…
Tomorrow's another day!
Time to pack the bags an',
Follow the sun.
Get some air beneath your wings.
I hoping for an afterlife…
No bands of gold
No bond of love
or chains of hate,
No reminders
to make
My life dissipate!
Whether heaven or in hell?
I might meet you with the angels,
If I'm late for the re org…
I doubt I'll see you in heaven.
As I've shared paradise on earth with you.
And I've got table booked for… 600 in Valhalla's hall!
When I feel I'm crowded… it's, because of my brothers!
Just say that you knew me,

If they care to ask about me.
Tell them, That I loved you deeply… Though,
even you did not understand me.

Does this to me sometimes
(mmmm perhaps a lot!!!)

123) Don't Cry

Write me a piece of poetry
While you hold me tenderly
And whisper it… in my ear
Just so you can…
Say goodbye to me,

Then I'll just become a memory.
A mere interlude in time
Of a moment where we spent it
as one.

Have another sip of your wine… it will help wash
away your tears.
Please try not to think of me.
For while… when I have
drink it's not, to forget,

But to remember… for it was…
A majik mystical time, of dreams.
Of frosty breath and crystal-clear nights

Where we talked of stars and mythical beasts
For me it was good… and,
Whichever way, I hope that it was, good… for you
too.

I'm just not worth it.

124) Images…

Cherry blossoms fill the air
As logs, spark… on an open hearth.
Release my spirit... to the wind.
Where it may mingle…
in autumn's… smokey airs.
And bring me hope, that…
In the spring, once again,
I'll hear your laughter, long
Before, the summer comes.
Let not my tears, wash away…
The scent,

of my true love.

125) I'll Never Be

You're in my head,
and in my heart.
and I hear your name…
upon the wind!
Where happiness
Measures in tears,
Of joy.
I cry, forever…

Over you.

126) Loneliness

It's...
The saddest,
Sound…

I know!

127) Truly

Empathy.
is embedded… in my soul!
I hope one day,
You take the chance.
To just… stand still.
And truly,
look around…

I'll miss you.

128) My Love

Hummingbirds hover,
While butterflies dance
Bees, waltz through the meadow,
To the sounds of silence!
Long grass, forms a long past…
That hides, fallen dreams.
As dusk falls, moonbeams call.
Drawing fairies, from their beds.
As the owl, sleeps… overhead.
Glow worms light the way…
For playful voles, and mice.
Majik fills the air, while you sleep.
And everything, I love…

is gone.

129) Have They All

When I awoke,
It was dark.
My light, had left my life.
Moonbeams… chased after,
Shadows.
While pain, filled my heart.
As apathy silently pummelled
My soul
Sorrow, had finally…

flown the nest.

130) Hush Please, Be…

My heart was full.
My chest, was tight.
My eyes, began to well.
You smiled…
And kissed my cheek.
When butterflies dance
The world, becomes one.
Time stops, and the earth…
Stands,

Still.

131) They Say, For Me... It's

You're a long time dead.
Life, is for the living.
True Love… is eternal.
Passion, comes from the soul.
While angels watch,
and weep…
for me.
And then… there is... you.
A butterfly danced.
And for me, there is… now

Only… you.

132) Please…

Please, take my arm.
Take a moment of your time.
Please, walk with me.
Share a moment of your life.
Please, talk to me.
Make, my heart sing!
Please, let me kiss you…
Make my dreams come true.
Please, fulfil my life.

Please, please me.

133) The Dawn Brings a New

I know more, than...
I'll ever say.
Mere prescience!
Proves that.
My hunger, only abated...
By your thirst.
I am sated and you...
Have, drank... deep.
Let me hold you, util,
The... morrow's

Morn.

134) To the West of Plato, It's

A vision…
Which changed, my life.
And truly, the lady boogied.
Yes she did…
She mesmerised me.
From the first time,
I ever saw her…
I experienced, a true love.
And I wanted for,
No… other.
A moment, in my life.
That eclipsed, all…
That had passed before.
True,

Bliss.

135) I Miss...

I miss that... laugh!
I miss, your... smile.
For, in essence.
I haven't seen it...
For a while.
Although, I have your picture...
On my wall.
Dreams 'n' memories...
Are, all... I have,
Of...

you!

136) My Relationship? It's a Bit

While loneliness…
Is the biggest killer,
That I know.
I seek a kingdom!
Within… my sleep.
Where my true love,
And I, dust go, to meet.
For, with her…
I shared a moment
Which, for me… has lasted,
For all eternity.
Where I have found a heart,
That is too big.
And thus, I cannot cope…
With those, I truly love!
It's just as hard, to understand.
And…
To try and escape, my earthly bond.
For I,
Look too far…
To far Beyond.
And simple things,
Become… for me.
Too

complicated.

137) A Distant Memory?

When… it's grey
I want to walk that beach.
And I'd love to hold, your hand.
Silver puddles… of salty water.
Glittering… upon the sand.
To feel, my heart lift...
Like a gull, upon the wind.
See your smile,
Dancing… in... your eyes.
To steal a kiss…
'Neath,
A chill…

December sky.

138) Time To Draw…

So, who would have…
Thought?
And, who would have…
Knew?
Apparently…

Lots!!!

139) As You Awaken...

With visions of a summer's morn.
As golden sunlight burns away... their misty airs.
First light.
Where colours hues...
and darkest browns... melt,
before the coming... dawn.
Dusty shadows,
now replace the dark.
And meadow birds... Now sing,
to their hearts content.
Beauty, fills my eyes...
warms my soul.
When I see you...

Stretch and smile.

140) It's A, Happy

Surrounded… by pictures,
on my walls.
Sweet memories, of a girl..
Who got me to dance!
Made me smile.
Brought me new meaning…
to life.
Remember… while you sleep,
That I love you!
Fear… gone.
In the blink of an eye, as you, dream… the night
away.
My love
Stronger, than… time.
Weighing heavily… forever,
Upon my heart.
Leaving tears, upon pillows… While our passion…
like,
rainbows.
Is never…

Ending.

141) You Just Do... The

You equal, all my dreams.
You solve… the sum, of…
All my fears.
You are… the answer… to
My equation, of life!
It's just, simple…

Math!

142) Someone To…

…
…
Love me!

143) Because We'll Meet

I masked… my hurt,
Within your scent.
In truth… I ask.
What chance, had I…
Worldly wise…?
Only in death... It seems.
While time, moved… on.
Flowers bloomed, then…
Died.
Love stayed,
within its bounds.
Nurtured…

in my dreams.

144) Breathe Deep...

Lover.
Whilst it's still free!
No strings attached.
Suck it in...
and dig deep,
While you can.
For Love's forlorn.
I'm trapped in this life.
Your world continues to turn,
And my true love is lost.
All in the midst of time...
And all I am left with is,
A mere shadow.
Which is etched upon...
My heart, burned in my brain.
I'm a victim of that,
Thing...

We call life.

145) Love's True Heart Is

Another year has passed.
And my memories… sit.
And gather dust!
While in my futures past,
Tomorrow… struggles,
to see the light, of dawn.
Dark, as is, as tempest… tossed.
I have no fear of dying.
I transcend.
For I am…

already lost.

146) Each Time

When I see you,
It's like a symphony…
Invades, my soul!
It warms my heart, fills… my…
very being.
You make me… feel alive.
Your cheeky grin, that…
impish smile.
The mischief…
That lights your eyes.
My taste,
upon your lips…

Is like no other.

147) Might I

In those downy,
dusky folds.
A silent, river runs.
And I dabble…
in the deep.
Drink, my fill…
and nearly,

drown.

148) Love

Such a simple word.
Which at times, can fill one,
with mixed emotions.
Ecstatic, Euphoric... beyond belief.
Or fearful... beyond all...
comprehension.
Empathic to a fault!
But no understanding, of... rationale
I'm honest to a fault.
And I'm afraid my fault,
Is...

my honesty.

149) Once Upon A...

Eighty-eight... to the minute,
Upright and true.
I marched, amongst the throng.
Forgetful... of you.
No futures my past.
Memories, never, meant to last.
It's all about her...
Not about you!
Her name, like countless others,
Is written, forever,
in the sands...
of

Time.

150) Truth Be Known,

I don't do lonely…
Very well.
Perhaps it's because,
I've been told… love,
is not…
An area… of my expertise!
Love for me, is hard to find.
I do however… love
pretty things.
Love… beautiful
people.
I…

Love and miss you.

151) It's All Been For

I took your hand.
Then held you, close.
From your face, I brushed away, your mousy hair.
I've shushed, and kissed your lips!
I've seen that haunted look,
Once, upon… your face.
It lay within, your eyes.
Those darkest diamonds… blue.
That sometimes… twinkled,
if you smiled.
Or when caught… unawares.
Your beauty was,
Enough… to make me,
Catch my breath.
And steal my heart…
from out… underneath me.
A true measure of my love.
Wild passion... and,
My desire, for…

You!

152) Hypnotic

Like little buttons,
Soft…
Like marshmallows.
That rolled…
On your tongue.
Sweet… 'n' gentle,
To the…

taste.

153) Alone

My heart has flown.
I survey… my kingdom?
No fortress, just solitude.
I long, for what… I cannot have.
I've no domain, to oversee.
Silently, I pine for you.
With no raucous laughter,
to subdue.
I sit here… all alone,

Missing you.

154) Say No...

Nudge, nudge, wink, wink.
I miss...
your elbows.
Our... winking,
games.
And all.. the bits,
In-between.
Please Miss!
If you've had your,
Coffee?
I'd like some...

More!

155) My Soul Felt...

I cast a tear.
Into, that internal void.
That some call love
In hope
it heals
A broken heart
Which calls to me

A Chill.

156) Poetry Oft Can

Unknown by most.
A poet's lips,
taste sweeter than… miraculin.
And his kisses… linger,
even longer than a vampire's curse.
He uses words… more,
Potent… than, mere karma.
Though his loneliness… which consumes,
is more infinite than the universe.
His love fills… pages,
and the void.
In an overindulgent, abundance.
While life… passes him by,
He'll probably die, alone.
His words…
will,

Remain unread.

157) In A Darkened Corner

I kissed you.
Brushed your tongue,
With mine.
And we both, laughed…
It was, momentous,
an…
Epiphany.
A meeting of souls,
Recorded in time.
That will last…
forever.
In the windmills,

of my mind.

158) From Here To…

Perchance.
If I should ever make you,
Even for a single moment,
Be as happy now, as you...
Make me.
Then I should rest happy,
For all...

Eternity.

159) The Eye of The

Like a rubins…
You saw my body,
At its worst!
But had the time,
To show your love...
And I returned it.
I hope, I paid you more…
Than just, lip service!
For you, were… like,

A… Tiger.

160) Sweet, Blue

Perhaps…
Just sometimes.
It can be more,
Than what we say… a lifetime.
Other, than just a moment.
Or longer…
Than a mere perception.
True passion…
Never dies!
Well not until… it's truly…
Recognised.
Though… It may just be?
A wish… lost,
Upon, a meeting.
Of…

Eyes!

161) Life's Journey

Perceptions?
Colours,
Moods…
Moments in time.
Missed, opportunities.
Moments sublime…
Wishes, cast on
Butterflies' wings…
Dreams, never drum.
Life's fulfilment…
It's made me,
Happy.
Somewhat… I'd like to think

Thus far.

162) Missing

I can't dance…
And you say,
I can't sing!
But… you catch, my love.
When I sigh.
And hold me… tight,
And… kiss my,
Tears.
When I cry,
Life's a dance…
And I'm dancing it,
With…

You!

163) Désolé, c'est le seul mot que je sais...

Sorry,
is the only word I know...
Which can be,
said... or written.
But only,
If there's someone to hear or
See.
Désolé,
c'est le seul mot que je sais.
Sorry,
Is the only word,

I know...

164) Just a Thought

Anyway.
You smell...
Of madness!
In an animal... kind of way.
Passion, oozes...
From your pores.
And your breath, smells,
Of cinnamon...
And your nipples,
taste like cherries...
Your essence, tastes of
Nectar!
And, I can never have...
My fill,

Of you.

165) It Seems Like It Was, Only

And when I saw your smile...
It was, a goddess, personified.
You melted my heart.
Stealing my breath away.
Ripping my soul... and,
Drinking, its essence.
With the coming of the dawn.
I was near spent... though,
You...
Were still there.
She smelled of rainbows
And all things majik
And she'd washed,
My pain away.
And I eddied
in her body's warmth
Savoured her dusky smell
Marvelled...
at her body's delight.
Felt... blessed.
I never, met you as a child?
Perhaps it was in another life.
No matter.
I bet... you were,
More than really wild!!
After all, you were...

Last night!

166) You've Got Hold Of...

At times,
You can run out of... love.
And, if there is no one,
you can feed off!
To replace it... Satisfy
The hunger,
The soul... can die!
My soul is now trapped deep within.
I have no dreams.
None... to share with.
Sometimes, we all deserve
a sprinkle... of happiness,
Take care, Blondie...
you made me smile today!!!
Brought a sparkle, to my eye.
And warmed...

my heart.

167) Deep Love and Feeling

There's a song, in my heart!
Who would've thought?
Of tumbling lyrics...
I'd sing, one day.
That all it took,
A Cupid's arrow...
In a millisecond,
It'd done its worst!
Now I'm forever...

Smitten.

168) Once I Was A...

Write for me, and sing...
a lovesome tune!
So, I can tell the world.
And share our words...
With more, than just us.
But... Now,
With all of them.
Like your laughter... your words,
They haunt my head,
and echo in my mind.
Screaming for a melody!
Lyrics born from a love
That was strummed on,
Tender heart strings.
And tugged a...

Lonesome soul.

169) Love Like,

Majik, never melts.
It merely fades...
Like a sweet perfume.
You've left uncorked,
It may linger...
In the echoes, of my mind.
Whilst I... tasted it upon,
Your lips, and smell it on
Your empty,
Pillow.
I want...

No other!

170) More Than Just Amber...

My tongue
craves...
to lick the bristles
of your,
snatch.
To push within,
Your sex.
To taste the hunger...
I crave so much.
To make you sigh.
To hear you cry,
And whimper, so.
To make you,
Come!
I miss, that moment.
Of when you arch...
And flood... my
Mouth.
With,

Nectar.

171) Gloaming,

She's the new love in my life.
And everyone...
Wants to know her name!
Though,
If you say it too... often,
It may lose its meaning.
But if you don't say it,
often enough,
You may lose your woman!
It was always the case,
That the ones that I wanted...
Were the ones, that were,
Gone!
Stolen by others.
Eloped like lovers...
Of the simple things,
In life.
A smile, a word,
or perhaps...
A kiss!
Baby Blue Eyes.
Fantastic... tits.
I was often, complimented...
On my ankles!
By women, that'd come to stay.
Of how thin... they are.

As we frolic' ed in the hay!!!

172) I Once Met...

Your inner, sadness,
filled me...
from your spoken words.
While birds,
no... longer sang,
Flowers,
lost their bloom.
Love failed... to shine,
For me.
On,
My beautiful...

Girl.

173) It's Been Much More Than Just

I like...
living in my memories,
Of you!
Missy... I Love you.
More than words, cards,
or flowers...
Could ever say.
For me,
the ride... has been more,
Than just...

Emotional!

174) I Spied You, An Angel

One winter's eve...
You came into my life.
Stole my heart,
'N'... crushed my soul.
Filled a void.
And while... I
Brushed your lips.
Made me feel whole!
You brought... me
all my dreams,

all at once.

175) I Don't Want To...

While you're here.
You occupy space!
Physically, mentally.
By favour... and full of grace.
With love, and affection.
Perhaps, maybe noticed
by some.
More like, noticed...
by... a lot.
And possibly so.
Though I know... it's true.
For when here,
you're ignored by none!
But when you've gone...
You're still here.
And I see your face,
and it's hard...

To move on.

176) We're Not Mexicans But

Not because
You kiss better,
Than Julia Roberts!
Or you're sexier,
Than Sailor Jerry.
It's just because,
most of all...
K.I.S.S. ???
It's because,

I love you.

177) Don't Talk to Me...

Just listen,
For those romantic writers,
Who wax lyrical,
About flowers, sunsets.
And what scents... upon,
The breeze.
Unless you've kissed,
Or tasted... sweet nectar.
Looked, into their eyes...
As you've held their hand.
Laughed... until it hurt.
Or hurt, so much inside,
You cried!
You don't really know,
Anything

About love.

178) Thinking Of...

A hollow moment?
Perhaps...
When your pulse,
Misses a beat!
And your brain...
pauses.
So your heart, fills...
With a void.
And reflections, pass...
From mirror, to
Memories.
And a silent longing,
Overcomes...

You.

179) It Touches...

There's a chill wind.
On which, a whisper...
Rides!
I understand it,
Not.
Nor, can I fathom,
Its reason...
Nor, its course.
'Cept, it causes me...
Pain.
And fills me... with,
Remorse.
Laying heavy,
Within...

My heart.

180) I'm Weird, #Strange...

My heart,
Lay near my feet.
And the glamour,
Left my mood.
For my intention!
Had been,
Totally...
Misunderstood.
And apparently,
It's...
A little bit,

Freaky...

181) Just My Dream

And all that I want... ?
Is for you to be happy.
It's not much... to ask for.
Forever and Always!
Should it be in my power?
Or, if I have to ask the Russians
To shake the ice, from your bones,
Навсегда и Всегда!
We could stretch out
on the golden Spanish sands.
I'd be by your side
Para Siempre y Siempre

Forever and Always.

182) At Hell's...

My heart...
has caused a pain.
That others feel,
And I'm to blame!
Selfish, little boy
Who treats his love,
And her emotions...
Like, some kind of adult toy.
Grow up!!!
Before it's too late.
And my true love.
Runs... down the path!
And out... that
Open,

Gate!

183) Of A Broken Heart, What...

Why...
Does my head,
Hurt so much?
A pox, upon... this,
Pain!
No rhyme, no reason.
One,
who only knows.
It causes me to write in verse,
sometimes in prose...
But the pain.
Still,

Remains.

184) Stroke Me, I Want to Be...

I'm blinded.
For...
I've touched a Phoenix.
Who's, burned my heart,
And melted my soul!
Her beauty, has...
Scorched, my mind.
And now I'm lost!
For... I crave her touch.
I'm fuelled... by the hunger,
Of her, passion.
Which consumes, so much.
I want to be...

Burned again.

185) Cupid's Arrow, Is Dipped In...

Like sand or water,
It trickles through my fingers.
Pray...
What chemical reacts?
Do pheromones,
Attack?
I'm lost, it's made me
Blind.
And all that I can see,
Is you.
And I never ask,
Who, Why, Where or,

What?

186) I Never Really Loved... Until,

Missing you more...
Than cards or flowers,
Could ever say!
More than I thought,
I could ever do,
For another.
That was...
Until.

I met you.

187) Come Feel The,

I'm in Love...
I have a malady,
That's froze my brain,
And stopped my heart.
Je crevé...
Whence thawing tears,
Cleansed mortal...

Pain.

188) It Smells Good...

I loaned you my sweater.
Not wholly, because,
it was cold.
But so, I, could wear it,
Later.
When you'd gone home.
And I would still
smell, you.

On me!

189) Me N,

I've been good.
N,
I've been bad.
I've been happy.
N,
I've been sad.
I've been a prince.
N,
I've been a Pratt.
And all the while,
You were.
Just,

You... N, that!

190) Finger Licking Every...

I've run my tongue,
the length of your body.
I've kissed you...
head to toe.
I've fondled, your flesh,
And I liked it.
I've kissed you,
all over!
And probed you...
with, my tongue.
I've tasted,
the dew drops...
of your come.
As it moistened, your lips.
From the centre,
of your being.
I've sucked, your nipples,
and...
your clit!
And enjoyed... .
every,

fucking bit.

191) I Love You, Cause You're...

I wanna barbecue...
on a beach.
Run,
along the sands.
Frolic,
in the waves.
I wanna hear...
you laugh!
I wanna see...
that,
twinkle... in your eye.
I wanna spend...
All... my time,
with you.
Having,

Fun.

192) Lust, Thirst's...

I've drank...
from that well.
And dipped my fingers,
in that, honey... pot.
Truly its fruits, tasted...
so sweet.
It put nectar...
to shame.
And love's addiction,
Now claimed, another...

Victim!

193) Love and Affection, Only

To hold your hand,
To simply touch.
An outwardly...
Visible sign,
Of my affection.
Chill,
I miss you...

so much!

194) I'm Feeling,

Once upon a whence...
I whooped!
And then,
I whooped again!
Whoop whoop!!
And life, was...

Good!

Well it is half past three in the morning. What do you expect? Lmao.

195) Perfect...

They don't, have to be...
perfect.
For we know
As we grow up,
and... or
When we're older.
We realise nothing,
is... perfect.
Everything,
has a... flaw.
Sometimes... though.
It's the imperfections,
we treasure most... in our

life?

196) Lover Of...

Call me on the morrow.
At the coming, of the dawn.
After, you have... stretched!
When the sleep,
has left your face.
And that pixie smile... has lit the room.
As just, to remind me...
That you're,

Mine.

197) Angel, Or...

When it's light.
I sense... your presence.
Through simple, smell...
And touch.
A warmth... of,
Heart and soul.
And whence, it's night.
A devil in my head!
While yet, another fragrance,
That lingers...
Which fills my bed.
For me, to sleep alone!
It would be...

Alien?

198) Be My...

Hearts and flowers,
Champagne.
Chocolate, coated...
Strawberries!
Lace, and lingerie.
Sweet... gifts,
From me, for
My...

Valentine?

199) One Of Life's

I chased that dream
For all that it was worth
But it was not to be
For once again
My inadequacies
got the best of me
And I

failed.

200) The Janners Are,

I harbour no illusions.
My experience
and age
Has made it so.
And I wished...
But I had no dream,
'O' overall.
For me... .
I Breathe the conviction,
Of your Eyre!
I struggle with life...
I worry,
that I'll never see... you again.
Never hear your voice
Or see your face
To hold your hand
So as I watch that,
Lady in red!
The bare-footed... Spandex dancer.
I think...
Don't forget!
To breathe,

In...

201) I'm Only a Human

Though.
Once again...
I feel,
Your frustration.
Understand, your pain.
Mere words...
from me?
Are all... that I can offer.
Inadequate as they
Seem.
But I send them,
from my heart.
With all,
... of my

Being.

202) We're Not Strangers...

When will we.
Share...
Our,
Erotic dreams?
Hungry mouths,
Consumed... with,
Passion.
Lips...
That previously,
Had only kissed
Over a telephone.
Now touch!
Hurriedly to bed.
To live...
That dream!
I'm not,
Asleep

Anymore!

203) Yours Burn, While Mine Are...

In the vastness... of the darkness.
I reached out, for you...
But once again.
Like my dreams,
You were gone!
But I cried...
Only,

Silent tears.

204) All My Love...

You want him back!
That guy, in the picture.
The man... on the wall.
You want me... to be,
Him.
Once again!
And I'd do it...

For you!!

205) Lucky...

Who can say?
Not I!
For your beauty,
Has mesmerised...
Me.
Forsaking all,
I am lost...
Deep within.
Your,

Charms.

206) I Stood...

and watched
Like warm rain...
The water fell.
A shower,
Can't you tell?
Slow moving...
Soapy lather,
Slowly, sliding,
Past rosy nipples...
Downwards.
While I
Watched...

In the door!!!

207) I...

I am, like no other!
I have a gift...
She is, my lover!
She keeps me...
Me real.
Down, to earth.
She is a gift,
Like, no other!
Because of her
I...

Am blessed.

208) Time,

is what I have an abundance of.
She called me...
"Sweetheart"
And now... my heart's,
Upon a cloud, within my chest.
Wrapped in glittering rainbows!
And sparkling eyes, and mischievous grin
Are etched within my brain,
And burned upon my heart.
For she also said...
"I love you"!

When it comes down to you.

209) There Is But...

Time and distance!
Which, matters not.
Whilst in the land...
Of dreams.
But soon,
She shall reappear... once again,
And be mine!
And mere distance...
matters not,
and neither does, the time.
For until she is in my arms
there is,
Only...

One Sleep.

210) Shush...

When, YOU, say it.
Sounds...
A little bit,
Pervy!
And when I...
HEAR, you, say it.
I know it,

Is...

211) I Was

just happy
that you seemed
to be happy.
My heart
only sang for you.
And I thought
nothing more
and time
meant nothing to me.
While
I was

with you.

212) I'm Forever...

I fell in love,
With a photograph.
That justice...
Gave no merit.
For in the flesh,
That childish...
Impish smile.
Though had already
Captured heart,
Stole it, away forever!
And I am lost...

within you.

213) A Chance... of Love

Mixed emotions.
Marred, by painful memories
Which stopped her heart...
A heartless fiend.
Who tainted, her love's dream.
With shallow thoughts... for
Sweet, fair maid.
Whose eyes no longer smile,
Perhaps... about to change!
For
A gentle knight would like to call!
And restore her faith.
Crush the pain,
Make her a true...
Woman.
Once again

You know you want to...

214) Let's Keep It In

Time and space...
While a world watched.
Two mythical creatures,
The Ryujin and the φοίνιξ.
Came together, on a majik web.
Where they began to dance,
A mystic one... of

proportion!

.

215) The Ryujin And...

I'd love to be there with you.
In the shadows, near your bed.
Silently watching...
Whilst the buzzing, fills my head.
To reach out and touch you.
Caress that secret place,
I'd stroke you with my thumb.
To see the pleasure...
fill your face.
And sink deep inside you
As I moulded to your soul.
I'd caress that φοίνιξ egg
While I plunged into that hole
Soaring heights of...
Frenzied passion.
The Ryujin,
And...

The φοίνιξ ...

216) Shhhhhhh

Say not a word...
I want to hold you tight
No... I lie
I want to crush your body
Close to mine
I want to flood you
Full of... Emotion
I want the heat from your... thighs
To warm my heart
I want to kindle a spark,
Sometimes just saying
I want to fuck the arse of you...

Just isn't enough.

217) Love's Blossoms

That her tears...
did burn deep.
And how your tongue... can lash
To seal that void.
And heal,
a wounded, warrior's heart!
Rest... those sweet lips,
that I have yet to taste.
Shush... .
Mine's full of death and pain.

But full of promise...

218) Bog off, Two For

A pretty girl,
Who is now a lady.
And who, has always been!
But never saw, within that glass.
Our worlds collided ...
Survivors, of broken hearts.
And as Cupid, let his arrow fly...
we clung together as

One...

219) If You Parked Your... Body,

Could I kiss, your sweet lips?
Could I hold , your body...
close to mine?
Would it be a chance meet?
A moment in passing...
Or a planned moment in time?
Would lust, win over love,
Or would there be a blossom...
That I could cherish?
Savour, and refine.
Would you put,
Your sweet lips...

Next to mine?

220) Faint Heart Would Never

I cried for one,
Far away.
Words, had all... but,
Failed me.
And I could only,
Imagine... the taste,
Of her sweet breath,
That kissed a Cupid's arrow.
One day he'll take another shot,
To cleave your heart asunder.
True love, will finally find its merit
And we shall... both

Win the day.

221) Chill

My fate...
Has been cast... to the winds.
No longer, master, of my destiny.
I await kismet!
That fair maid's...
Farewell,
Didst break.

My heart... my love.

222) Truth Is

I'm more fragile,
Than you know.

223) It Skipped a Beat...

There was a light knock,
at the door.
As I opened it...
Framed, in the doorway,
Stood a siren!
Pure sol
And my heart... Hammered

Within my chest.

224) Hey Chill, Whatcha

Poems from a tortured mind
Or mystic ramblings
from a troubled soul
While a pensive lover
Like no other...
that,
He's ever met,
Holds his hand,
And his heart.
His pen is still,
Though he's ever...

Thinking.

225) It's Not Cupid's Arrow

You went and... stole my heart!
Then you ripped it,
right in two.
We'd spent the night together.
But now that the morning's, here.
What else...
are you gonna do?
If I even tried to run,
Would I make it out that door?
I'm so darned confused
I don't know...
what, to do

anymore!

226) Go For It...

I'm Alice.
For me it's...
Mirrors no longer.
I'm looking,
through... the glass!
Like the vampire
The mirror... has no soul.
A mirror only reflects,
a moment in time.
Why sit and stare and look?
It's a waste of time.
Life is for living...
Not reflecting.
You do that just before you
Die.
Valhalla's a long way off...

YOLO!!!!

227) My

Lost love,
like the seasons...
change.
The next...
more memorable,
than...
the last.
Though it could never,
replace.
True...

love.

228) Where I Have Walked

I have... walked
Mombasa's,
silver sands.
I've trodden,
To the North...
on the darker ones.
In Africa... In Sudan.
I've seen a φοῖνιξ
mate a dragon.
I've heard... .
A Ryujin roar!
I've heard the sensual mew...
of a φοῖνιξ.
I've walked where,
No man's walked...

Before.

229) Merry Christmas, Breast Or

There's a new love...
Which brought sweet chill.
That's touched, upon my heart,
And other parts... !
Of where I've drank my fill.
Sweet sighs...
Escaped cherry lips.
As I lapped nectar,
Deep...
Between her,

Thighs.

230) Some Men Have Women...

I'm happy.
Though I miss you!
I miss your... musky scent.
I miss your... gentle touch.
I miss, my kissing...
the smoothness,
of your mound.
To lick the valley, 'tween... those breasts.
To suck, the pink perfect buttons

that dominate them.

231) Good Morning

I'm feeling...
Myself.
But I'm thinking,
Of...

You.

232) Ryujin

In the cold grey light,
of a winter's morn.
Sweet φοίνιξ slept...
In her earthly form.
Watched over... .
by her Ryujin.
Whilst...
in her slumbers
A regal gold,
φοίνιξ glowed.
in time...
with the breaking,

of the dawn.

233) Ryujin Slept

While...
Sweet φοίνιξ,
Came to him...
in a dream.
The dragon stirred...
And so Ryujin
Lost his heart.
Consumed...
by the

fiery φοίνιξ

234) It Always Ends... In

Your scent...
has now been washed,
from my loins.
Nor does that heady smell,
Still linger!
Though my heart... is
Still raw.
And my soul... still,
Smoulders.
From your fiery,

Tears.

235) The Sweet... Taste... Of

I'd like to,
dabble... ,
my fingers,
In your honeypot.
Watch life's juices.
Dribble... from that,
Slot.
Breathe deep.
From, your excelsior.
The source of,
Pleasure... To
Lick my fingers
Suckle... your
Breasts... be a part
Of... your,

life!

236) *What I Want Is...*

I'd love... to,
feel your shoulder,
lean on mine.
Intertwine our fingers,
Hold your hand...
Feel your body move,
as you breathe.
Watch your breasts...
sink and rise.
See that little vein,
in your neck... pulse.
Feel your body's warmth.
Touch your soul.
Steal your heart.
Oh Vienna!
I'd love to...

Chill.

237) Speak Now... For

I shed a tear... for,
foolishness.
And the silence,
that I kept.
Which caused...
my true love,
To be...
forever lost.
And so

I now languish alone.

238) My Dream Lover...

She's like a drug...
I can't get enough!
And I can't... stay away.
She's captured, my heart.
And I'm hers... always,
And...

Forever.

239) I'm Thinking What to Do

I can still,
smell myself,
inside you!
The night's passion...
still, runs deep.
All we did, was share a bed now.
But darling, I got no sleep.
Let me, meet you, once again!
And before that night is through.
I'm gonna do...

Crazy, mad things, to you.

240) How Restless Is

Waning moon's, pale light.
Lit a path... unto your door.
Which welcome-lay, lay ajar.
Nectar's scent, lay
heavy... 'pon the air.
Her eyes,
reflected in the light.
Showed
Love's, heart's passion.
And thus,
Worked majik... so.
He stayed...

The night.

241) Always...

Clutched to him tightly...
a warrior, held his maid.
While sun shone,
Upon a rainbow bridge...
I heard today,
and did feel your lash...
that made, a dragon cry.
As tears dug deep...
They cast a shadow,
When thence a φοῖνιξ's breath
Brushed my warrior lips...

My fair lady & true.

242) Love's...

It's not for me.
That simple quiver,
In your voice.
The twinkle in your eye,
That breath of sunlight...
Upon a spider's web,
Tis for another.
Who lays dark
Within your heart.
And holds my love,

A prisoner!

243) Wet

Wakey... wakey,
Sweet kitten.
I'm home, once more.
While lost dreams lay...
Crushed, upon the floor.
For
Daddy drank with Vikings,
last night!
He ate all the leaves, from...
Læraðr.
And now, he'd like...
To claim
His prize... I hope

Perhaps it's still moist.

244) Why Am I

I'm listening to the radio
and I've heard a song
that's made me cry
It made me think of you
And of all that I was missing

Nature's ganging up on me
The sky's the colour of your eyes
The leaves the colour of your hair
I swear to God
I smell your fragrance in the air

All I'm left with
are memories
Life
Is so fucking unfair
It's you I want to be with

Alone again?

245) Clandestine Meetings...

A telephone... is a mere,
Conduit.
To another place,
Which steals...
A moment of your time.
Via voice, and buried wires,
Where dark secrets may linger...
Or sweet secrets, of promise,
Can be murmured.
So a date, a rendezvous,
In the dark of the night...

May take place.

246) Don't Worry...

And all that I know,
Is you've been hurt,
Many times before.
But I'm here... .
For you now.
I don't need,
To know...

Any more.

247) Without Love

They say,
That there's no fool,
Like an old fool!
Lucky with money,
Unlucky in love!
I can truly see, why...
Or how.
People go nuts.
They're either starved,
For emotion, and love.
Or, they are so full of it,
They can't give it away!
Only the lucky ones,
Who live in-between...
Never dared, to venture,
Never sought, paradises lost!
Mr and Mrs Mundane.
Eros, remove your arrow, now!
I can take no more, of this pain.
Just make me...

normal again!

248) Hey Jock ...

Each one...
Is vastly different!
Though the effect,
May be, just the same.
Grown men cry.
Jump off bridges,
Lie down, just die...
Intangible, non-fathomable.
It rules your head,
It can crush your heart.
An overpowering emotion,

Love.

God only knows why we have it.

249) Such Sweet

What heart
Of any man
Could but deny
A blown kiss
From a cherub's?

Lips.

250) I'm Here

I just want to hold you tight.
Kiss your tears...
Make things right!
Wash away your pain,
Make things better again.
I want to be by your side,
I want to hold your hand.
I want to be there...

For you.

251) All That I Know Is...

I see you in the morn.
As you stretch,
Stifle a yawn.
Curl up again,
And lick your lips.
I've seen the mischief...
In your eyes.
Felt your body's warmth.
Touched the heat,
From your thighs.
Tasted that probing tongue.
All the while,
Just
Knowing...

You were mine.

252) A Whirlwind

Bright eyes, mirroring blue eyes.
Where dreams have met the shore.
Life's expectations, turned to sand,
Toto, it ain't Kansas, anymore... !

Romance.

253) I'm Mixed Up Baby...

I misinterpret, daily,
My lover's... thoughts.
And perhaps... sometimes,
Her dreams.
I never seem,
To comprehend,
Of what, she really
Wants or needs.
My heart is hers...
And should she
Choose to listen.
It beats with a will,
and a passion,
That's for her

All, Alone.

254) Let's Do It...

I kissed my love,
And she replied...
In kind!
And the heat from,
That passion,
Melted...
My heart.
And I was,
A man...

Again!!!!

255) I Love Your...

I just want to...
Stroke your arm,
Cup your chin.
Kiss your...
Cheek!
Pinch, yer...

Bum!!!

256) Me And,

You have that something...
That, I don't know what?
That...
Je ne sais quoi?
That unknown quality,
That lies underneath.
Below the surface,
Unseen...
Like the North Pole,
Magnetism!
An animal attraction?
In a simple, pure,
Demure... kind of way.
All I know is...
I've been,
Drawn... To

You!

257) I Like to See You

Sigh!
One of satisfaction.
Of happiness,
from you...
It's,
a dream...
of mine.
To know...
You've been,

Fulfilled.

258) Once Again

I've seen...
A rainbow!
And now,
I believe...
in fairy tales!
I believe
in majik!
For,
I've found myself...
A princess!
And I'm
So totally...

In Love.

259) My All...

And if I had one wish...
I'd wish for you!
And if it were a dream.
I'd only dream... of you!
And if...
I'd had to forfeit,
my meagre life?
I'd gladly give it

for you...

260) Babes...

My words are all
Terms of endearment.
Signs of affection.
Expressions of... love.
It's to let you know,
You make my heart sing!
I can't help it...
I'm glad and I'm sad
that at times,
You think

I'm freaky!

261) Technology...

Who said, love's dead?
It's the new age.
Connecting lovers, via...
an electronic,
world-wide... web.
But it's got tenuous peripherals.
And it may sometimes, put ideas...
in some, unhealthy heads.
Causing, untold pain.
That's often shared,
in a dot com, kinda,
public... domain.
 Faster than a Cupid's arrow.
Love... splits the night.
But sometimes too,
it goes the other way.
And when turned off.
The cache...
Can be

Dumped...

262) I Miss... Sharing with You

Love's scent, and it hurts... so, much!
Nature's beauty, and its wonders,
Pale... in the wind, and can't, compare.
Would a rowdy, sugar glider, glean... more love, than
a, lonely...
bearded, dragon?
Please don't break, your promises.
But try, and, keep... the dreams real.
For, would I really, wish... to know.
How does the Kinkajou,
perform

in bed?

263) I Love the Taste of

I kissed a girl.
Sweeter than nectar,
Who tasted...
... all woman!
My soul is like my heart
... I felt the urge.
And I kissed her once again.
I kissed a woman,
More potent than wine.
Who was, my... Girl.
For once upon a time... in

A fairy tale, or make believe?

264) Bed for Me, Sweetheart

Maybe a warrior has other skills,
that may prove to help fair lady?
Dream of me,
and perhaps...
I might dream again,
and see you there.
Smell the beauty... of your soul.
I hope I get...
to hold your hand
Taste... sweet lips
I truly hope I do.
I hope, I get a chance
to see... to,

Sleep with you.

265) Your Essence is on My Mind For

There's sadness playing on the radio.
But it matches a song in my heart.
Of a time I heard you smile.
When music, was your laugh.
While tears still roll, they wash my soul.
As they drown, the sorrow in my heart.
I miss you more each day.
My thoughts are full of love's hunger.

My body craves for thee.

266) On the Sands... I Saw Her

At Saltburn on Sea.
Where, winter's silver-grey waves...
Rippled... along that coast,
and out to sea.
A pixie-hatted beauty.
Stood... halfway on a hill.
Twixt me, and the shore...
Hand on hip, and...
A twinkle, in her eye!
And I see her even now.
Remembering...
How I loved her,

Smile.

267) An Answer, Which I...

The warmth, of my heart,
Is here, to hold you.
For... I have no more words!
Just love.
For I am mute... and
Perhaps... only.
Deaf ears...

Now await, for me.

268) Forever... &

With a tear,
And a...
Sigh!!!
Missing You...

Always...

269) My Thoughts, Are All A...

No matter...
where, you are.
Or what...
you, think of me.
I'll always...
think, of you.
And I'll...

dream.

270) Perhaps One Last

If I asked...
Would you, taste my lips,
One last time!
Would you, share, that smile?
That... broke my heart.
Let me, smell... beautiful.
One last,

Time.

271) Dreams

I want to fly the pond.
Kiss the sun, at the meeting...
Of the dawn.
See Manhattan, by night!
Take you to lunch.
As the breakers... roll,
On that golden Venice Beach.
But your love for me... like,
My passport's
Apparently... .

Expired.

272) Ne Jamais dire Jamais

Not ever...
Just walk away... instead.
My world, has touched
Where time, emotion, and love...
Have no place.
And I... am not a part.
Never say...
Never,
Again!

Ne Jamais dire Jamais.

273) Kiss Me... I Love Your

Passion.
Locked,
deep within your psyche.
Was your love, touched... upon my call?
Did my words, soothe...
a ragged heart, or quell,
a hidden rage?
Did I see... a glimmer,
of a flash!
That lit your eyes?
And made you,

Smile.

274) Binned...

I kissed my angel
Who stole my heart away
And left me with
a troubled mind
And now I lie in limbo

... ?

275) They Fill the Night and I See

I, have learned...
Love's, lesson.
Which has left,
a chill...
Upon, my heart.
A fiery trail.
And though I weep... it,
Has opened eyes, so... wide.
My breath is hushed and...
I can count, within the sky,

every star!

276) A Lack of Words Has Been

Perhaps,
For those we love.
Not necessarily, a bugle's call.
But we'd still lay down our life,
for each of them, or all.
To share a breath,
or hear their heart.
Of that special... one,
We sometimes meet.
Aaaaahhhh!
To not disclose this eternal love.
But rely upon a whence.
Perhaps, has been...

My mistake?

277) At Hell's...

My heart...
has caused a pain.
That only others feel,
And I'm to blame!
Selfish, little boy...
Who treats his love,
And her... emotions,
Without scant thought.
Grow up... mate!!!
Before it's too late.
And true love
Disappears...
out that,

Gate!

278) The Very First Time

My happiness lies, within...
My past.
Last night...
Last week...
Last month...
Last time...

I saw you!

279) I Pledge...

Not if, but,
When...
When I'm dying, lover.
Share me... a mirror!
Before I pass.
Then I'll see,
What you've seen.
I'll see...
What I've shared.
With you.
In that mirror.
I'll see...
Within my eyes, that mirror
Of

my soul!

280) Expectations of a Weekend

Do you remember
when, it was fun?
When you actually...
looked forward to,
meeting up!
Expectation... prior to,
exhilarating... fun.
Love's, blind thoughts.
Heightened by...
copious amounts,
of alcohol.
And the possibility,
of a...

Shag!!!!

281) For Me...

To hold your hand.
Or touch...
... your tender cheek.
Or stroke that flaxen hair...
And push it... from your brow.
All for a chance,
to gaze, into those eyes.
To see my own Sjöfn,
There I'll breathe deep,
To taste...
... your musky scent.
While marvelling at...
your glistening skin.
Of...
Tiny beads,
... like honeydew!

That tasted of... love's nectar.

282) Use Words, Tell Me How

Conceptual

I am.
Don't quote me, semantics...
Don't... paint my portrait.
Don't, sing my song.
Sketch me, a... landscape.
For all my life's a... musical.
Ever meet me, in the morning, when...
Egg shells, fill my brain!
When I've chased, the magic dragon.
That haunts, my dreams.
After, I've watched, a lover's moon, sink.
As it waned.
After I'd watched life,
through, streaky... sunlight.
Reflected, on green, tinted windows.
And when, the last red balloon, had... gone.
I'd see,
the writing... on the wall.
What price

is love... ?

283) Hush...

I'll listen to your words,
no... more.
Would the swans, regally frown,
Or compromise, my love?
I love, chiffon.
How it holds, and touches,
as you move.
Of how your body rustles.
Should be, that I meddle.
Would my life fade?
Should my death!
Herald the dawn...
Or make,
no sound

No more...

284) I've Found... Perhaps

I saw.
Within, your smile...
I saw, a hope.
And so... I held you hand.
That, then led, to a hug.
That led me, to kiss,
And I kissed...
An

Angel.

285) Je Ne Sais Pas...

Who knows...
And I guess I never will.
I don't know of this feeling.
Or, where it comes from.
How it descends to crush.
Or how, it briefly, lifts... my heart.
A sadness of euphoria, that only those, that have felt
it...
Know.
A full-fulness, mere words... can't, describe,
or an emptiness beyond, comprehension.
At times I cry and cannot move.
At times... I can dance, like... Bruce Lee.
The winter's winds, they oft bit me, deep.
Freezing my bones, right through.
But, it was a brief, breath of, fresh air.
A hint of a chill, that that went...
Straight, through my soul.
The winds still find me, wherever I hide.
And the sun...
fails to bring warmth, to my being.
My spirit has flown.
All my happiness gone.
Save my memories
Which are now, fading.
I'll sit by the fire, in the great hall, of, Valhalla.
Where I'll slowly roast my bones
And I'll learn a new song to sing there.
So if you're coming...
Along
Please tell me.

286) It's a Little Lonely...

I'm missing, a little company.
On cold, winter mornings.
While, glistening... frost melts.
And on, those balmy summer nights.
When, summer's scents... fill the air!
They say... love,
will find me, once... again!
But I fear... she,
knows not

where I live...

287) Call Me, If You're Looking For

I'm not elusive...
Just a tad, reclusive!
Because, you've left me...
Wanting,

more.

288) The Mystery of Love, It's

For all the women
I once, loved...
And of those, I never... told!
I hope deep down, you just knew.
For I never got the chance to say.
On lonely nights when tears do flow
I often long... For.
Well... I don't know.
Perhaps... I've still, a chance?
Before I die, for...
one last

Romance.

Just let me know...

Who's, now being teased,
with that wistful smile?
Or those wicked, sparkly,
come to bed eyes... ?
Those provocative lips
A look, I once knew... well.
Albeit too briefly.
And gave me, artistic license.
Terpsichore, you led me, a dance... But.
You
filled, me... with,

inspiration?

290) Unless I'm Told...

You,
have caused the tears.
Which have washed,
my soul.
And I miss your touch,
So much.
My heart is squeezed, within a breath.
While death...
is standing, on my chest!
And I know... no other.
Nor, their bewildering kiss.
Vehement or

Otherwise!

291) When The Time Comes

We are, all... alone.
Lost... Amongst, the crowd.
Meanwhile.
I'm drowning... in happiness,
as the alcohol, goes down.
Lonely, is a... state of mind.
While love, is... a longing, of the soul.
A brief interlude, that lit my life.
Forbidden fruit, never tasted so sweet.
But, you broke, my heart.

And took my breath away.
So I've learned,
in the end

Hypoxia gets us all...

292) Pray Ignis Fatuus, as Foolish as I Am

I'll not be back, this way again.
My path lays beyond, destiny.
So go to sleep, sweet child.
Morning will come, and I'll be gone.
Dreams fade and dreams die.
While some, never grow old, beyond the sunrise.
I was, the glimmer, in the shadows.
Today, will be liken, to yesterday.
Like, I was never here, before...
I'll just be, that forgotten memory.
A lost voice, just...
Talking, down the wind.
Once I was a melody, you thought, you'd heard.
A flicker in your smile.
Now
I'm just a little piece.
Of smoke

a wisp... ?

293) Que Sera Sera, Whatever is Meant

With each simple man-hug.
There's...
A little part of me.
That's purged, from, within my soul.
I'm, slowly dying.
For
I miss you, each, and every...
single day.
And nothing, fills this void.
And, none... will, ever see.
The widening hole, within, my heart.
Where, you,
once...
Used

To be.

294) My Lust, Like The Tide, in Waves

Consumes me.
I want more, than to just... look.
I need more, than just...
a whimsical smile.
Misty eyes, and wistful... sighs.
While, thinking... of you.
Just kiss me, and say no more.
Let me taste, your lover's... bite.
As your darting tongue, tastes... my, love.
Let the rising passion, tremble, in your thighs.
Let me, wash your soul, with... waves, of emotion.
I'm trying to feed an emptiness
All the while, your touch...
makes, my body... sing.
Beneath the calm,
a storm

is rippling in my veins.

295) Pass Me a Cigarette I'm

Once again... I tasted,
That evening air.
Trod, those steps,
Upon... a silent stair.
Darkness glowed,
In shadows of green... luminescence.
I sat upon a lonesome step,
And wept.
The wind rushed by
... taking tears.
It shook my soul,
... rattled my bones.
I wanna kiss, a dream...
That's gone.
I wanna be

The skittle man.

296) A Night Fit For

Hang up your hat... put away, your broom.
Drain the cauldron, candles... well just,
snuff the flames.
Until next year then, to weave... your spells.
Don't let the pumpkins rot.
Ghoulish sighs emulate...
From darkened rooms.
Nobody... visited my drum.
So I never got to,
Bang

A witch.

297) I've Run Out Of...

Don't brush away my tears...
They're full of pain.
Of broken promises, and dreams.
But they're all I've got... of you.
Memories, fused... within my soul.
Let me kiss... those cherry lips.
Nibble, on that neck.
One...
Last

Time.

298) Waiting... For Phone a Call, From

While snowflakes gently, fall...
and swirl, in and out,
amongst the trees...
Nature's ballet, plays unbidden.
Its total majesty, rests... unseen.
I heard the lonely robin's song,
I don't think I'll wait, for another.
As too many tomorrows...
Have already, passed... my way.
So I hope the devil...
saves me from the sunrise...
For the moon, has...
Stolen

My love!

299) Love is Never... Drowned By

Stifling heartache...
I have the time.
I have, the knowledge.
But not, the inclination!
I'm happy that you've found, your someone...
I'll just lock away, my... memories.
And smile, all the while.
As dust clogs my heart, and masks my eyes.
My life enters another form
Of Lonely
While my tears, remain.
Neither,
Happy, nor sad...
But just

Tears...

300) He Always wins... Does

My heart is tainted... and...
I know not, why.
I live a curse, of lost... loves.
Of love, unrequited.
Perhaps a victim,
of a long forgotten war...
Of hearts or...
When death, split... the night.
La petite mort... Meant more!
And love, lasted... longer,
than an interruption... by the dawn!
And I'll ever remember, that... last kiss!
Your caress, and a dream...
Now long past.
And long, forgotten.
I linger, and only wish...
For

Death.

301) Thoughts and Dreams

Just some, perhaps, not... all.
A mere few.
Todays, and yesterdays.
Good... times, bad... times
But I'd trade em all, for
Another shot with you, in the morrow.
I smelled,
a long-dead, stale... cigarette.
I saw the heavens lit
By stars, that are, no longer there.
I felt my heart stop.
As I sighed for a love, I'd lost.
Who tells me to shush... ?
When time, has run out.
When, there are... no morrows left.
Who then, ends...
the dreams

Of an old man?

302) I'm Now Deaf, Where Once

Love has opened my eyes...
but closed my ears,
I seek amongst the stars...
a whisper, I once heard.
And I've closed my ears, to stop...
any corruption of your voice,
so it echoes in my heart...
and rambles pure,
... throughout my mind.
Drifting... amidst memories.
Of late-night cigarette smoke,
that mingled with the wind,
as I stood and watched a love,
I've now lost.
For now, I'm deaf...
But once

I was blind.

303) I Miss You And...

I'll see you in Japan.
There is an essence lingering... within my mind.
Where a single word,
may have meant.
More... than my life's breath!
All I can do now,
when I think of you
is smile...
and

I wish you well.

304) I Miss... to Kiss the Corners of

On sleepy, Sunday mornings.
When there's nothing, happening.
And folks, don't do... much.
I, miss you...
I miss... my love,
I miss your... touch.
I just miss...
To hear you sigh,
For me to admire... as you lie.
Your body... from head to toe.
To share a coffee.
Bask, in the shadow...
Of

Your smile.

305) A Lonely Lover Full Of

God save us from the sunrise!
And those, that share, that... drunken bed.
Save us from... life's mysteries.
Only bring... sweet dreams,
And alcohol...
Induced

Amnesia...

306) Lost in Limbo at...

Some point.
I thought I heard you call me.
In that blackness, that is... the night.
'cept... I was alone.
... Your ghostly, touch.
A scent that lingered...
That scent, was... you!
So
While in the depths,
I heard you... cry
In

Gehenna.

307) A Pain Which Fills My

There is a Candance
which flows... through,
my soul.
Setting, the rhythm...
for my heart
While, I stood before, Kandake.
It stopped, and I was lost!
No anthem, have I sung.
And while I wait the dawn,
Its beat, has slowed.
I know you sleep.
But... I'm bothered by,
Your troubled mind.
Which, has caused,
My affliction...
... My... troubled,

Heart.

308) I Look at You but, I Can't Say

That, the tightness of your dress
Has really, made... my day!
And, I am young again.
Full of desire.
With thoughts that, well...
Perhaps.
I'm more tired, than I seem.
For I find no solace,
from my dreams.
My joy, is solely mine.
For, there's none here, with to share.
Short lived, and epiphanies... of life!
Soon forgotten, and buried deep.
Don't let me, lie lonely.
Would spiders,
therefore...
Kiss!
Before they dance, upon my grave.
Would laughter fill its web, awhile.
And I... for.
I've cried those Russian tears
Once too many times.
My silence,
will... I keep

For my thoughts, may get me jailed.

309) *Trust Me,*

For...
I have indeed, felt the rain.
Sweet, warm, and gentle.
Like a feather's touch.
An intimate caress.
An everlasting taste.
What colour now,
is
your, dust... ?
Never trust in faerie tales.
Nor a twinkle in an eye.
I have that, kicked curs.
Empathy... and
Its... total, incomprehension.
As to why... and,
why me...
And yet like that cur...
I came back for more.
Ever loyal

I was a fool to love you.

310) It Waits For No Man, It's The

Kiss me before I sleep
A time to treasure
A moment to keep
Of a place of where we'd been
Of a time of who we were
I saw the sea
I smelled romance
But I failed my lover...
Now she's left
On the

Tide.

311) To Glimpse, Your Smile As

I couldn't... just,
hold you,
or,
Not touch you.
In any, asexual... way.
I want, to... dominate you.
But not, in any,
kinky,
kind... of way
(Unless, you want me to... that is!)
I want to hear you sigh.
And see you blush... as you
hide your face,
While making that, kitten whimper...
kind of noise.
I'd bring you love, with a touch.
Give tenderness, with a kiss.
Show my affection, with a smile.
I'd take you seven ways to sunset.
And,
I'll still be there,
When

You awake.

312) Another Victim of Zorg's... One

Feels...
Sorrow burns deeper
Than, any flame, or ember.
Though my tears, were wet,
They fell, like dust.
I could have been.
So, much, more...
But, you never,
gave the time,
nor,
Me, the chance.
It's only frozen words,
that now echo.
Not,
that chill

of romance.

313) Everything... Dies... Except,

... Love.
For love, merely touches
The hearts, of the... living.
It has, no soul, of its own.
Its known, to be, a sentimental affair.
So it, drifts... constantly.
On the winds,
of

Romance... everlasting is love.

314) Still Waters Run...

Within a world where,
A sigh, that cuts so deep...
That bites.
And fills my heart, with grief.
With pain, which echoes in my mind.
And fails, to make me sleep.
A hush that covers my world.
So I hear, each teardrop...
as it falls.
While love's whispers...
Cause a sigh.
And cut...
Me

Deep.

315) Merched Real

Yr wyf yn cofio pan fydd menywod yn gwisgo menig,
Stilettos sodlau uchel.
Gwisgo suspenders gyda hosanau.
Roedd gan bronnau a oedd yn real.
Cyn mewnblaniadau colagen,
PMT a'u cluniau cellulite.
Mae menywod a oedd yn feddal i'w gyffwrdd,
Gyda cynllwynion benywaidd
Bywiog a melys
Cilwenu a swil.
Atgofion melys o blentyndod,

Pan oeddwn yn fachgen.

316) My Butterfly

Summer's gone
It has finally flown,
As it left its wall.
Nature, caused its sway.
I opened for it...
A window.
On a stormy, autumn day.
And it

Left.

317) *Pan ddaw'r glaw Down i mewn,*

Mis Hydref, trwy mis Chwefror.
Byddai'n ymwneud... gaeaf.
Ac, cofleidio... dan cwiltiau!
Er bod y dail, syrthiodd... o, y coed.
Wrth i ddiwrnod niwlog, troi i mewn i,
nosweithiau tywyll.
Ac, cusanau... tyfodd yn hwy,
na'r dyddiau!
Byddai'n ymwneud, plu... Ac hufen iâ , ac...
toddi, ciwbiau, o rew.
a
cyboledig i fyny

taflenni.

318) Sadness

Rules, my soul.
While my heart, lays waning.
I miss each touch, and every kiss.
And still, my body... lays, wanting.
Love.
Never, more... I'll be.
Not, once more, will I see.
And while my lips, crack, and chafe.
In dreams.
I only think, of those, long... dead.
'N' kiss, lost... forgotten lovers.
Only ever thinking, of the past.
So my wish, is, not... to dream.
For my past, is my future.
And, so, it... remains.
Tomorrow, will be, yesterday...
While today, will ever be,
The day preceding... My death.
While
An emotion

Stole my soul...

319) Wet, Damp Or

Something in the air...
Smoke... ?
On the wind,
it
Brings, a melancholy... taste.
That pauses breath, stops a heart.
Brings, the echoes... of, the dead.
I have to learn, to once again...
Smell the flowers.
And only listen, to the...
Whispers,
Of leaves,
on swaying trees.
To hope that my age, and dust.
Won't affect my mood, nor my eyes.
And if it does.
Then they...
Be left

Only... slightly, moist!

320) Sitting...

Listening to the rain,
Brought forth, a memory.
Of a life, I'll never see again.
Of places, and lovers'... faces.
Long gone, and flown.
Of growing old, in another's arms
Loves, lives, and mystic charms.
My life's passed so fast.
Like my women... it seems, and none... remained.
Perhaps,
I'll leave this world
Like, I arrived

All... Alone.

321) Just

So you know.
I love you, more...
Than the blue,
that fills
A summer's sky.
Or floats, within... a sea.
I have drowned, in the depths,
of your... blue eyes.
While, the sound of your voice,
has made me... swoon.
And, all I know is, I'm...
None, the wiser.
But, I'll always... come back,
To

You.

322) Immeasurable, Beyond...

My, understanding.
That, in nothing, can compare.
Mere words, giving, no justice.
Unwritten, but told within the stars.
Love.
Unfathomable, incomprehensible...
Inexplicable, of who, chooses who.
Where those scorned, have no voice.
Remain invisible, mallow, Pedanius Dioscorides
named you well.
For I see you beauty, and breathe, your par-fume.
Inexplicable

Are my dreams.

323) I could taste her,

Scent.
Through moist lace, and silk.
Where I'd gently...
Nibbled, and probed.
Her thighs still hot,
from my touch!
As her mons, rested on my chin.
My ears, were full of flesh.
And I heard not,
those satisfying sighs.
But felt her arch,
and quiver...
in her passion.

And... It made me smile.

324) Save Me, a... Speck of Light...

Some, prefer the darkness,
and the singularity.
Though crave, the companionship, and the warmth,
that...
another's voice, can bring.

But, fear the rejection, should they ask.
Soon
I'll run out of memories, and
I'll just be... alone, and lost, and... bitter.
Love, in life's, an act...
And at times,
Too hard

For me, to follow...

325) Once Constare, Now You've

Stelan
If, I could only
steal, one... kiss.
I'd be, just one touch, before
euphoria.
And, I'm left wanting.
My heart is sār, and piqued.
I'll dream, of... death.
For his embrace, is constant.
Unlike those, who've shared my bed.
Gone when it is light.
There are no rainbows after dark.
There are no colours in the night.
And memories fade to shadows.
And even your scent
Is

Gone...

326) In My Secular World...

Who hears a lonely heart?
When you're all alone.
Could a single drop of sorrow,
Turn a lover's tide?
My tears, have ceased to flow.
Each day is like the last,
While tomorrow's... like today.
No reason, nor rhyme, just a waste perhaps... of time.
Once upon a Cupid's arrow
I was sent, a lover's card.
I breathed it deep,
and my breath... held.
While tears, moistened my eyes.
An epiphany touched my being.
Of never, nevers, and of what... might, have been!
Sweet dreams, of a sweet lover.
And in my heart

I cried...

For Jackie Hamer because she asked.

327) Tears Like Water...

I turned a page,
Within a book.
Where... only pictures were.
And a thousand verses,
Filled my eyes... and
It

Flowed.

328) I'm Thinking of Death, Ever

Never, ending as,
God only knows...
For an emptiness,
fills, my being.
For on this night...
I'm full of sloth, and envy.
Drowned, in forgotten wishes.
Which now...
Litter, the floor.
Laying, amongst... empty cans,
and dead... vodka bottles!
My tears, burn my eyes.
My sobs, wreck my chest.
Crushing... are my thoughts!
Sublime, are the memories
Which surround me.
Ever enticing...
Ever... closer.
Ever

In my thoughts.

329) Neothan, My Love Drifts...

Like those,
who crossed...
The bridge of sighs.
My heart, too,
is held a prisoner.
I'm kissing shadows.
That have been left, to
Linger
In forgotten, corners...
Of, my mind.
Unlike... those,
that passed, beneath.
My love, is...
not

Eternal.

330) Good Things, and... Love, Yet

Look beyond my words, to...
a mood, once there.
Now long gone.
Which echoes, in a soundless scream.
Like the beauty, of a jewel, or a song.
That can be shared, but is ever only, meant... for one.
In unguarded moments, I saw
Desperation,
in your eyes.
Like an innocent child, with...
Dreams.
I'm living...
Back, in yesterday... once more.
Waiting...
for you

to come... tomorrow?

331) Once Upon a Dream

I ran like the wind,
with the devil, at my heels.
I never knew,
what... luck,
really was.
And now it seems,
I've used it all...
So.
Share with me, your... eyes!
And let me... dip, into your soul.
I'm searching for, that little, sparkle.
Which lit a flame, within my heart.
And burned me, to the core.
I crave a hunger, that I once had.
For, life...
For, love...
For...
A woman.

Now long gone...

332) I Never, Ever,

Got the chance, to... say.
I loved, the way, you... moved.
Or...
How, the sparkle, of... your smile.
Touched, your eyes.
I held a breath, too... long.
Not saying, the words...
You longed, to hear.
I heard, your, soul song.
And I stumbled, on my dreams.
While my tears roll, for,
a lost... romance.
It's your voice
I long, to

hear.

333) I'll Carry On, To... The

Point of no return where
I'll still walk,
those... lonely roads!
Looking... for that light.
While, I may stumble, perhaps...
Even fall.
I have to ask... .
Am I searching for, the... impossible?
How can you, measure... an, emotion?
Who says, love... even exists!
What is lost, within the depth. Of...
Now, deadened... eyes.
Where lustre, fails to shine.
Like the cosmos...
Pain.
Can be...
Without

End!

334) The Truth Twirls, In...

Spirals...
Like time.
Silently the seasons change.
And I watch...
In awe and wonderment, of nature and,
her phenomena... at work.
As I see how her qualia, just abounds!
Lost in the melange of colours,
from falling, dying... leaves.
That, swirl and flutter, on the winter's breeze.
To come to rest, in trickling streams.
Then later, as those red, yellowy, colours... fade like
rust.
Be... now, hidden.
'Neath a downy blanket
Of fresh, sparkling snow.
Turning, the once, colour-rich, landscape,
To white, with flecks, of blacks... and greys.
The epitome, of an English... winter's day.
Like an ageing lover who's...
Grown old.
Their dreams now black, with mould. Being left to
rot... And crumble.
Like autumn leaves, turning...
Eventually

to dust.

335) I've Heard It... And It's

When a dead man, sings.
And it's sweeter, than...
Life itself.
Where time
Has no limits, nor... conceptions.
When music, fills, my... being.
Let the music, move you,
like it, sways... my soul!
There is no glory, in dying.
There never has, and never will!
So live today,
like, there's... no tomorrow.
Live it wild, and
live it,

loud... !

336) Me and My...

Was it... the wind
I felt,
upon... my cheek?
Or did,
a long-lost... kiss.
That caused, an ache...
Which, burned... it,
went so deep.
It crushed... My love.
Each time, I... weep.
And so, it shrank... my heart.
Each time... that it, was broken.
And... it is now... but,
a hollow...

Shadow.

337) Directions, to the Road of

Licentiousness...
From the murkiness,
of grey, and black.
A hand, reached out.
And closed, my eyes.
My silent scream...
Long, lay dead.
And thus, I was, now...
On the road.
Of

Dreams.

338) Oh Woe,

Who hears, that silent... scream
That fills, your eyes?
Who, starts... that Chinese, whisper?
That's... full, of lies!
What fool, can't... comprehend?
It's back, to spider... solitaire.
And tear-filled nights!
I languish now alone,
Once more.
For, that...
Fool
Is me...

339) I Couldn't Cry So I...

The mist parted... Before me.
Swirled... Around behind me.
Filled, the void... I'd created.
I strode through the night!
The mist, death... and me.
Hollow, eerie echoes...
For each, near silent...
Footfall.
Like a spectre from the past,
Lost souls willed me on.
Even more wished me ill...
And they all

Laughed.

In a Gallic, kind of way.

340) Oneirology...

Have you ever been
Where, it just seems, and... It feels just right!
Where a thought, upon a sigh
Has meant...
A love, deeper than... well.
More... than, just... passion.
When with you.
A mere moment, a speck in time, goes beyond...
Infinity.
And from brief touch of hands,
Lips meet and a kiss...
To cause a lust, that would... free pent emotion.
Open
All the locked doors, of the seven kingdoms.
Send a surging tide.
Spare my thoughts of you.
To think of me...
For, have you ever,
shared

a... dream.

341) Chun Comhroinn, go Nestle

Feicfidh mé a shealbhú tú sábháilte, laistigh de... áit.
Go ach tú, agus mé, beidh a fhios.
Agus beidh mé aoibh gháire gach, agus gach, lá... go
awake mé!
Le haghaidh beidh mé ag mothú, do teas, laistigh de
mo lámha.
Agus mo chroí, go mbeadh osna... le mise.
Tá sé an rithim ar, i info, le mianach.
Agus bheadh grá fan, ag... flaithis geata.
Mar a bhí againn cheana féin, fuair
True grá

Hairm a chéile.

342) Emotions, Nil By Mouth, Nor Any Passed...

Within the darkness,
You were my light.
And now...
I'll dream, and, not... know.
Alcohol, fuelled thoughts,
That turn to dust, spread, on the wind.
Though, no mere squall, is this...
for Coriolis, has spoken.
What, with the dawn, remains... still fresh?
Or muddied by, a forgotten taste.
'Twas you, who said goodbye.
But by deed, and...
Not

By word...

343) Adieu? ... It's

Immortality... and a trick of the light.
I'm saying goodbye... to old friends.
And I'm having problems...
Understanding... what's my dreams,
And what's my reality!

Farewell...

344) Time To... Just

The irony of my life, has always been lost on me.
My soul, is loneliness,
Unable to share...
While my heart, once filled with love,
Has now, all turned to stone.
Lead lined, with apathy.
Time to

Say goodbye.

345) Farewell Goodbye...

I don't wish, an angel to,
Speak for me!
No polka dot shirt for clarity
No obsolete dreams...
No test of destiny...
I'll meet your expectations,
With a smile and a curse.
My life has piqued!
And for that...
I wish you

Adieu.

346) Here's Saying Goodbye

Draw me, a wish,
'Pon... a whitened wall.
Where words are, clear 'n' strong.
Rock me... a lullaby.
My children, will sing.
Colour me, a value
That will last, after I'm gone.
Paint for me... a dream...
For I am,
Blind

To it all.

347) Catch a Sunbeam...

Perhaps life's flash,
As you pass on by,
Doesn't happen all at once!
But through a short period,
Of random thoughts!
Of whence life was good.
And the moment evokes...
Fond memories,
Of whence life was full, and
There were no consequences.
The flash is a rush of fulfilment
As you try to catch the sun.

Before it sets.

348) Of Love's Spiral, Which

A princess... of the storm?
Sadness follows me, like a blackened cloud.
Smoke... from a broken heart.
And who would know,
And who would care?
But only you and me.

As the breath of a winter's dawn
Washes...
Chill... morning, mists... away.
Lethargic spiders, drink
from drops of dew.
And I realise,
I can't... compete.

I've heard it said, but never knew.
For death has claimed,
my lover's heart!
Who would be my queen,
And who would be my fay.

Lover, meet me one last time...
On a misty, winter's day.
When the sun's, long gone.
With only stars... to light my way.
A first, my own true love.

Hear my words,
straight from the heart.
And who could say,

that I never... ever, loved you?

For a love... unannounced,
nor proclaimed.

Remaining...
Merely in my heart...
where, to this day,
It still remains.

Who knows...
From where it comes?
That black cloud...
which hides my love.

Like a curtain,
It

Descends.

349) I Once Had Someone...

If you're lucky...
Sometimes,
people... touch...
your life,
As they're, passing through.
Sometimes, they may sit awhile.
Perhaps... even stay.
Sometimes...
For... Forever
or merely, for a night and day.
Whichever.
They leave their mark.
And misty eyes, may follow...
A pained heart.
For theirs is the path.
While wonderment... merely lays,
at our feet
That...
While we were here,
They chose
us

To talk to.

350) We'll All Meet at the FRV...

I feel a need...
for the sound,
... of laughter.
For... I've now run out of tears.
My life, lays strewn... in my past.
My heart lays, in tatters...
like my banner.
And my destiny... lays,
at the portal of Valhalla.
Behind an unknown door.
Paratroopers don't die...
They go to Hell,

And regroup!

351) Par Cause De

And, what do I know?
I ain't no hero.
Just a forgotten soldier
That society, has left behind.
And, what do I know?
As the seasons, change
And the wind, starts to blow.
While the rain, and its puddles
Clutter up, my mind.
And, what do I know?
Why tree moss always, faces south.
And seven lengths in front
Will always take a mig down.
And, what do I know?
Love can be fun!
But, it can also be cruel.
And 40 proof...
Can wash, your memories away.
But, only the good ones.
Just a broken soldier.
And I say these things,
Because

I know...

352) Perhaps Today's, The...

It's just for me, and,
I hear a call...
from, those long lost,
And those, just gone.
With whom, I share a bond.
Lost souls...
Brave men, brothers true.
Which creates a longing
Which fills my heart.
Which is a love-spurned void.
And their calling,
Gets, that little bit louder.
Every single...

Day!

353) Because Neuroanatomy Left Its

There is a sadness... in my soul, that does not, reach...
my eyes.
Nor mirror, in my smile.
It's only shared with nature, and the stars... when, the
moon... is full.
Or I feel, a...
Spider's

touch.

354) A Rainbow's Colour Has No Black, Or

Where did the colour come from
That now fills the trees?
Was't we a-slumber?
And it happened in our sleep?
Or are we just blind?
We seldom see,
Nature's, wonder, of what surrounds.
As life's omnipresent darkness
Keeps one's, head, permanently... bowed.
We become oft, blinkered, and so miss.
But, on we go... each day.
Feared to look up, to check the skies.
Hunched, and scurrying.
As we wait.
For the sound...
For the screams...
For death... to visit, kill and maim.
Eyes void of dreams.
Which now only see... All life.
As black,
And

White.

355) If I Gave You Flowers, Would You Be

Stolons... Buried or adventitious?
Could the stamen from a lily
Colour one, so deep?
That its scent...
becomes indelible, a stigma,
to your
thoughts... ?
Ever been so... sad
You couldn't sleep?
While I...
May not, be getting any younger,
I know of those, who won't grow old.
Sometimes
because we think, we know,
We don't say...
And a moment, is lost,
for all time!
Thus regret,
casts a wish...
That, no one, will collect!
If a song, could cleanse soul,
Would you sing one,
For

mine?

356) The Birds And...

My heart, is torn.
For, I feel its pain.
And, such is the hurt,
I may never, love... again.
Too look, but not, to... touch.
While beauty's scent assails my
Senses.
Life sometimes sows,
Wanton seeds, that only feed... love's lust.
To leave
A hunger, that... consumes...
Too much!
So as such... I'll only sit, and maybe look.
For... Now...
I'll stick to the beauty of flowers,
And their

Bees.

357) Goodnight, My Love, My Lover...

Who's now, with another.
I smell seashells, I hear the wind.
Once... I trembled, at your name.
While you, quivered... at my touch.
I long, for something, someone.
I've long forgot, that taste, of love.
Nurture, me anew.
Let me help, chase you, a... dream.
Let me, chase you.
My long-lost, and...
Forgotten

Lover...

358) Love's Passed Me By

Until someone saves me,
from the dreaded amber nectar, and...
Red, red wine.
I fear that I may drown.
So, for now...
I'll keep singing, my Swedish ballads.
Not understanding, nor knowing why.
Perhaps, one day, I'll seek... a translation.
If I ever wished, to share a sunset
Or to say a word,
Who would empathise with me?
Love's a curse...
When ignored,
when, cast in the shadows.
When it falls, on stony ground.
When it is

unrequited.

359) *Cariad*

Come the night.
I see your face, then... drop, into that, murky well.
The darkness, descends, and all is gone.
An angel touched my heart.
I smile, and then... I'm asleep.
My love, will keep me safe.
I dream now, only for... the, morrow.
For, my memories... make me, weep.
There's a hardness, to me, this morn.
For your love, had touched... my soul.
And, I... am
Now

Reborn.

360) Butterflies and Rainbows on

Goodnight.
Hollow... as it may ring,
You've, touched... my heart,
and...
struck a chord!
That shall, forever...
sing your name.
Just colours... etched,
Upon

a rainy day... ?

361) Poems, of a Forgotten Soldier

The old man's writings...
Love poems, sonnets, and of other forgotten things.
Read by many.
Understood, by a mere few,
though none of them read... by you.
Misplaced affection, having lost its direction,
now faceless, with time.
The sound of a voice... giving no choice.
But... they're not the words,
that I, long to hear.
Kisses... sweeter than wine,
forgotten with time.
Softer, than a faerie's touch.
The emptiness I suffer,
Through the lack of caress, upon
Your silky soft skin.
Memories and moments
Where a floundering fool,
Let his love slip away.
Remembering...
The poetry she brought into his life.
The glow it brought his heart,
and its grief.
Just know, they are always written...
from the heart.
But not all are written
in the mud, and...

initialled by death.

362) Of The Living And The...

They say, that the dead, don't...
Talk, back.
But them, that said... that.
Don't know!
For I hear them, in my head.
Some say, their piece, and... go.
Though some, choose, to remain.
That's them, that's scared, and lost.
The ones that, just... don't know.
That... they're

Dead...

363) Old Men and All of Them Are

Brothers...
I stand now beside them.
Though,
I only see, young... faces
Of, fresh-faced boys.
Not, the wizened ones.
Full, of the ravages of war.
I still hear the laugh, of those long gone.
I, remember, their now... forgotten... deeds.
And tears still flow, for those, of long ago.
Of when, we were young.
And I stood...
Amongst

Warriors.

364) I am drifting in a non-world, towards...

Where none can see.
Where loneliness, is the norm.
Where silent smiles, are never seen.
I'm living 'neath, I know not what?
Ever slowly, dying... inside.
Colour me, and kiss my love, for
I sigh the condemned man's, sigh!
A life within, where there is no hope.
Where nothing, changes.
Where nothing, matters.
There is, a nothingness...
To both the predawn, and last light.
It's only in the middle.
Where life lives, within the light.
And all, are too busy, just to see.
While, all the while,
Endless dreams, float skyward.
Stealing from us.
Small pieces, of our soul.
And I long, once again...
For
Happiness!
Hoping that it's...
That light, at the Tunnel's End.
And not

That rainbow'd bridge.

365) I Walked the World and Now I'll

Remember the four continents, where...
I've stepped in grizzly bear shit...
Watched, a penguin...
Have a piss.
Seen...
Skies so clear
I could touch, the stars at night.
Felt a monsoon's rain...
As it cleansed the streets,
Saw raindrops... turn to steam.
Watched fields, turn back
to mud, once again.
I've crossed dusty desert plains.
Ate jungle snake!
Drank...
Where dusky-eyed maidens...
Waved, and smiled,
with an... Innocence
Which belied their years,
And their trade.
I've seen the world,
From an inverted... vertical, terminal dive.
Smoked 'em down... dumped it low.
Watched the red...
... and done the green!
Watched horizons disappear
Felt the earth... Move!
But I've always managed,
To
Walk away.

366) Nyet

Zavtra nikogda ne nastupit
v techeniye dnya yeshch...
n am yeshche predstoit tantsevat'
ya zhil s lozh'yu ya nikogda ne videl
aa muzyka igrala pesnyu
so slovami ya nikogda ne ponimal,
ya byl zavorozhen vashey krasoty
i nichto ne imelo znacheniya

bol'she.

367) No

Tomorrow... never, comes.
For the day... has not, ended.
And, we have yet, to dance!
I lived with a lie, I never saw.
As the music, played a song.
With words, I never understood.
I was mesmerised, by your beauty.
And nothing mattered
Any
More...

368) Siol Nan Gaidtheal...

I breathe deep...
and your musky scent,
assails my senses.
... Tentatively... I reach,
and warm flesh meets my touch.
My eyes open... as I roll.
Meeting your, baby blues...
You've been watching me, sleep.
It's a moment, worth keeping.
I touch a finger to your lips...
To hush.
Too long... I've waited this meeting,
Savouring it oft... in my dreams.
Slowly we melt together.
For my mind is full...
of sand and dust.
The scenes of war with all its sounds,
of the... screams, of buzzing rounds
Of the dying and the dead.
My heart is yours, and I'm...
Lost now... .for the moment,
in the tenderness, of your caress.
Love's stolen moments...
A memory of lust... that lasts.

My seeds are sown.

369) Seeking a Singer for My

I'm not looking for an orchestra to play a symphony.
Just one voice, to sing my life's

song.

On a Volunteer Singer:
Swans sing before they die; 'twere no bad thing
Did certain persons die before they sing.
Samuel Taylor Coleridge (1772-1834)

370) Saying it, With...

Flowers... fade and die!
And petals... fall.
So
I gotta admit.
I've been, a little... down!
Cause, it's hard... to keep, smiling,
While
You're not around.
If things, could be... different?
I'd have back, yesterday.
I'd forget all about,
tomorrow.
It'd always be...
Just a, today.
But just like, you...
The colours have faded,
From my beautiful flowers.
And
Their scent is all gone...
My lover's dreams,
now lay, dying...
And so are,
my

flowers...

371) The Sun is Set, its Shadows

Come to mock me.
And I'm haunted, by your laugh!
It's good, to be wary.
But sometimes a brush, can cut a swathe... too wide!
And too... deep.
That clouds, our eyes, and makes us... weep.
And good men, rest alone.
Because of, one... man's
Vile deeds.
And so now, all tread wary.
For, the...
Nights

Are lonely... dark... and long.

Saz 15/26

372) Could Caesium Atoms Tell,

Just for a second...
And then... when
I heard your words,
I'd thought, that they were...
... mine.
Alone.
But now, I don't know... ?
I miss that voice, that... I, adored.
Only I can say, 'twere never a day,
That I never... thought of you.
While oft...
Sometimes, from the corner... of my eye,
I think I see you smile.
Then, I smile too!
Feeling... foolish.
For I know that,
you're no longer here.
That scent I smell.
That warms my heart.
And makes me, think of... you.
Is a memory,
From...
Another

Time.

373) I've Walked...

Lovelorn on...
Lonely... misty, roads.
Often, out of sight.
I've glimpsed, and briefly, tasted...
Love.
I'm lost, within a murkiness
That has lapsed, to darkness.
And I no longer, taste...
The, sweetness... of, my love.
Perhaps...
... she still waits for me?
Beyond that sea, and behind that last mountain...
I shall only know
If once again,
I go in search, for love, and...
Walk

That lonely road...

374) Big Boys Don't...

Share... A
... temporal perspective.
But...
It crossed my face.
And, I know not why.
Then, it was followed by another.
And,
I'd begun... to cry!
Who knows...
What, you're feeling
When you're hiding, inside?
For, no one... can know,
what... they can't see!
Unless, you

cry... !

375) Hear My Heart, Alexithymia

A word, I'd read today.
And, in not, understanding... it.
I was, a loss... at what to say.
Was it a word, known, to only, the young?
Or a forgotten word, of the old, and wise?
No matter, for it only made me, cry.
And, if I'm being honest,
I couldn't

Say... Just why...

Nome 08/29

376) Gucci

I have, no... palatial space.
No... grandiose mansion.
No... room, to play,
a piano... naked.
Or otherwise!
Four walls, however, big... or small,
Still echo empty, of your footfalls.
But, there... ever lasts
Within... my heart.
Your lingering

Scent...

377) Advection, An Equation...

When, a lover's... tears,
Have, no salt.
How fast... they flow.
How deep, they burn!
They turn to clouds, and...
Misty, teary, eyes,
Burn, with pain, as they...
Drown, a lover's dreams, and...
Block out... Romance.
Is it just enthalpy... ?
Or perhaps
Love's...
Equation

$$H = U + pV$$

378) My Eyes Are Teeming

Don't speak to me
of
Tomorrows
Nor mention, the things...
I've done, for... love!
Sometimes, it's hard
To follow one's heart.
For, we don't always get...
to, choose...
Our moments.
And all my dreams, now...
lie in ruins.
When I hear your voice, I die inside.
Don't look at me, like... I'm
a fool.
For though it's only, mere... emotion.
I have a talent, to make those I love... cry!
Devotion... has destroyed my life.
Distance, it is said...
Makes the heart grow fonder, but it also ages, and...
fills it

with dust.

379) Love Kissed Me, And

My heart is full dust.
As sunlight, dries... my tears.
I once heard, an emotion,
that, still faintly, rings... within,
my ears.
An angel said... she,
loved me!
And then

she flew away...

380) Similar Maybe, We're Not All

Some of us, write...
For those that...
That... do not speak.
Who merely sit, stare and weep.
For our, tears... are done.
Unlike, the others.
Who have, forgotten... how, to cry.
Their tears... are yet to come!
Each new day, may not, always...
Hail, fair winds, blue skies, and.. bright sunshine.
But.
It's a new day...
All

The same.

381) My Hopes Were Consumed, By

Failure.
I'm searching, for me.
For...
I'm lost.
Cast adrift... Alone.
Swept up... and, dumped, amongst, the throng of
humanity.
My voice, is trapped, within my head.
Though my soul, was long gone!
My heart, still... ached.
You made me feel... special, inside.
Irony, tinged... with, emotion.
Some words, resonate,
louder,
and longer...
than

others.

382) If I Meet You Again, On A

A day, just like... yesterday.
Don't tell me, that you, never... loved me...
For I know, that's just... a lie.
I touched your soul, in so many... ways.
But I know... too, that I made you cry.
If I could have just seen... tomorrow.
I know, that you'd never, have left me.
All I ever do, is dream... of you!
All I ever want, is to feel, your touch.
That I, could have lost, an angel...
It breaks my heart, too much, to say I love you!
It kills my soul, because you've gone.
I have no reason, for living...
You... were the reason, I saw each dawn.
Perhaps, I'll meet you... on that,

Stairway to heaven.

383) Hush Now, Go

And leave me be, for
I don't, sleep... so well,
these days!
I tend, to last the night,
and, see the dawn in.
For the dark, is... lonely,
and, I... dream,
no more.
And so.
I have, no...
Reason

to sleep.

384) Moods, Feelings... Of

Love...
Invisible, whimsical, wishes 'n', dreams.
Moments... that last, for all time.
Whether they be, happy, or whether they're sad!
For being just a memory... Both, can make you... cry.
But.
In a funny, fluttering heart,
kind of way.
And at the end I'll smile.
While thinking...
Of

You.

385) It's A Forfeit That I

Suffer and an amercement,
caused by Cupid's arrow.
For I may remain
Eternally... sad.
But, I'm not afraid... anymore.
I watch from behind eyes,
that have seen, more than most!
From where I guard,
a forgotten, lover's... heart.
Which I once stole...
In a moment of, wanton lust, and unbridled passion.
Happiness, lays... within,
true lovers' hearts.
While my love... is now cached, deep within my mind.
With tender memories, from, that majikal... Other
time.
Though you are now gone and fading.
There's a chill within my heart,
From where my melancholy grows.
For,
Some things, are, never... meant to be.
And love, has... a price.
That not all...
Can

Pay!

386) Left by a Lover's

A sinistral's touch.
When tears, just... fall.
As darkness, calls.
And love, has crushed, the light.
An old man, watches... lonely.
While nothingness, fills... the air.
I dreamed, a black, dream
That filled... the night.
And wished, that I'd...
Not

Wake.

387) My Dream Perhaps, But

I cried, for... I was alone.
And the couloir, was full, of talus.
I cried because...
All colours, were a shade,
too far... from, a rainbow.
And no one heard
Now I'm sad, beyond... all, measurable concepts.
To a degree, that only, dead lovers know.
And none, shall now soothe my fettered brow.
I once wished, and found... my dream!
But alas, I, was...

not hers!

388) A Word I Loved, Long Time,

Was...
When I heard you say.
Hello...
An innocuous, insipid little word.
That meant, the world... to me.
When it was said, by... you.
Said with a kiss, and
smile... in your eyes.
Said...
a long time

Ago...

389) In Love, or Life, or in...

All that I know.
What, I don't have!
I don't miss, anymore...
Well, maybe not... things.
But people?
Well people, they're different, of course!
I'm here, all alone.
And the silence of the night, has deafened all my
dreams.
Now all my celebrations...
Are of people, getting... older!
Of remembering, the... dead.
Of things... I once did.
Of what... you once, said.
And I've had, my fill... of life.
When we were, together.
I could... fly!
My life, was... full.
Now,
it doesn't seem real... anymore.
You're still here.
Though only in my heart, as... a fading, memory!
Just tell me...
Who signalled the end,
who, slew the dragon... and freed my angel?
I lost a dream.
I drank nectar... for,
I kissed, your

Essence.

390) Isolation... Imposed To...

Chill... A sharpened dragon's blade.
Perhaps... Kill love.
For I'm hidden...
From the shadow, of your warmth.
Though I heard, no other voice, but yours.
That only I, heard, that... which, you... whispered.
Yea only, I... did truly hear!
And, I'll treasure it, with tears... for, evermore.
As the snickersee, sliced deep.
And it cut my ties, with you.
Until that moment.
I truly felt,
my idolatry,
might

Never end.

391) I Dreamed a Little Dream...

And now...
I'll find a quiet corner
And wait for God... to
Explain of love.
And its, mystical feelings.
Why, tears fall.
And why, your lover's breath, tastes sweeter...
than, the nectar of the gods!
If I threw my wish upon the tide,
Who would now share,
my thoughts of love?
Do dreams, really crash upon the shore?
Or merely cause, ripples... on the sand?
Would they still remain, or... recede, with the waves?
I'm trapped, within a dream!
And a fantasy to, your devotion!
I need you to return, to set... me free.
Where dreams, are merely, dreams...
I wished, upon... a romance.
And it failed...
I'm cast adrift...
Forgotten

upon life's seas.

392) Did You Hear...

What, moves a moment,
To cause, a tear?
I fought demons, in the night!
Whilst, you were asleep,
Did the music, of my madness, intrude... upon your,
slumber?
Did you hear me cry, or see me weep?
Did you...
Feel

The somnolent effect?

393) Like a Smoky Spectre... But,

It's now tomorrow... Today!
Sleep well...
For love, comes in our dreams...
And disappears... before,
we wake!
But you... You, were real.
I held you close, I loved the touch.
Don't let the pain... wash, away... my memories!
For you

You warmed my heart.

394) I Can't Live Here...

Now... you've gone!
Too much here, reminds me, of you.
I won't... live here, now you've gone.
You broke my heart, and stole, my soul.
Each time, of every day,
serves a sweet memory of you.
I tasted love, and she tasted...
Sweet!
I hunger once again, for her touch...
I need you by my side, it's a love, I just can't hide.
Who will take me now you've gone?
I can't live here

Anymore.

395) Forgotten Music, Only In...

That moment, dust... touched, my eye
And I smiled... like I had once, long ago.
When I'd first found, new love.
Who said goodbye... ?
And who left, who?
You smelled of honeysuckle
And all things, nice.
Your body glowed, and your smile... melted, my heart!
What's not to love?
A touch that was electric and,
voice, that echoed...
in

my dreams.

396) Cold Feet Seek...

All the good ones... are,
gone.
All the great ones... mere memories.
Today
The air... is cold, and somewhat lacklustre, even old.
For I taste it, as I breathe.
And...
It's no longer filled,
with the sweetness...
that we shared.
But a stale hollowness,
That longs...
For the love,
Of

A warm heart.

397) Sometimes

things
happen, and
a moment, may feel
so good!
You want it, to last...
forever.
But.
We must always, remember.
It is merely,
a moment,

after all.

398) Would My Dreams Tire, Now I've

Wearied?
While my paranoia,
is a time-invariant.
It's running out of time.
I'd fill a fountain, full of wishes
To hear your voice once more.
Hey little girl,
will you remember me, when you grow up, and...
I've,

grown old?

399) Despair...

A black dream
That no one, wishes... for!
You've found me, at an ebb.
And...
I've yet, to see the sun.
Would that a cloud, could block...
Orionoid's visit?
Who, would trust, the voice of love...
If his messenger, has lost his voice?
Who sings

melancholy's song?

400) A Splash of Colour...

When all you have,
are...
lonely tears.
I'd wish, that I could play,
upon... your heart, encore.
For I would write a symphony, just for you.
But
Love has spurned me
for a bloom.
And now I watch
The petals as they fall
Dying, before the Arctic's
Snows

A winter's rose.

401) The Inability to Speak, Meant

Nothing...
Where do words go?
When...
They're cast upon the wind?
And...
How do spoken words,
heard, by a lover's... ear!
Resonate, so loud...
they make... a heart stop?
Was it you, I spoke with?
In the moments, before the dawn,
Was it... your, lips
That brushed against mine?
I woke alone, yet again.
But

I smelled you in my dreams.

402) So, What's the Point of Sleeping...

Feelings
Hidden... undeclared, life?
Living, in the shadows.
Forgotten...
If you're in love, and die,
Is it a love, that lasts, forever?
My tears, still flow
But are never seen.
It's not,
Oneirology

If you can't dream?

403) Precious Is My...

Lover
I'll not, dream tonight.
Nor dream tomorrow!
For, I never dreamed, while... yesterday.
Mayhap, there'll be a one
Who tells you, of what
I once did say.
And knows, my written words were all, for you...
My

Fay...

404) If I Succumb to Sleep I'm

Lost within.
The darkness,
has come, to claim me... yet again.
But
I'm too old, to die... alone.
Too old, it seems...
to no longer, share?
I heard a laugh, that brought a smile.
But you had gone.
I smelled, a whiff of perfume,
on the wind.
It smelled... like yours,
but you weren't there.
Once again, the night has brought... the memories.
I share alone.
For now, everyone...
Has

Gone!

405) *Animadversion Maybe, But*

I'll keep my love
for those
of you...
Of whom, I share, an... affinity.
Of those, that lie, long... dead.
But, meet me, in my dreams!
For a love, who is of flesh, and blood
Is not, for me, it seems.
A bond, of knowingness...
is what, we share.
While objurgation's not a game I play
And I point no finger
And

no blame...

406) Who's That Knocking at the

Gates of Hell?
Bring it on, for
I've tasted kisses...
Far sweeter, than wine.
I've seen eyes that sparkled
More brightly, than any star!
I've smelled love's scent...
in the early morning air.
Memories, more tangible, than
Mere dreams!
Of sight, and sound, and touch.
A love,
that consumed... so, much.
Now lays spent.
At, death's

Door.

407) Never Gonna

Well...
Maybe, one day!
But not, this... day.
Though a wistful tear, gives... ?
A secret moment, shared... with hope.
But it's spent, alone.
Is it in the air...
Or in my DNA?
Why is it, only fools
Who

Fall in love... ?

408) Smoke,

... on the water,
Smoke,
... in my eyes.
Smoke,
... to hide behind.
Standing in the 40+ something, shadows of life.
I've passed you by...
Long time.
... Before.
Smoke,
... dissipates to nothingness.
Smoke,
... is not, tangible,
Smoke,
... Like.
My, smoke

Like... corporeal dreams.

409) All I Want For Christmas Is...

A special friend.
A dear someone.
For once, it was said, to me,
We can still be, "friends".
And foolishly, I did say... no!
For I, wanted... more.
And now I've learned.
When, you are offered
A small piece... of the sky,
Tis better, to... breathe it in.
Rather, than asking... for it all!
As, that may be, just too much...
for some.
And more, than a friend
Is willing, to give...

You...

410) Desperately Seeking...

Peace on earth... !
Your demons, were not... my demons.
Like, oscietra... you left, an exquisite,
salty taste, upon... my tongue!
While irrumatio was your norm...
I loved it, when I could make you... smile.
Like the Myrtle, I've lost my Zoza.
So
Be careful, what you... wish for.
Choose your pebbles... well, for
There are
No

Perfect... dreams!

411) Outrunning Death, as Solipsism Plays

When's, the last time... you walked
Barefoot... In the grass?
Laughed
While running... in the, summer rain?
I have a need to share, and...
Time...
seems... so precious now.
But
Its all, in a rush!
Life's slipping, through my fingers.
Too fast, for my eyes to see!
And, I'm too weary...
to

catch up…!

412) If Tomorrow 'Twere

to be.
A better day...
Need I rise, this morning?
And, were I to risk, tomorrow,
Would it just become,
another

Yesterday?

413) Ó Dhubh Go Dhubh

Love's dorrain has left its scar on me.
There's a blackness,
Fills my body.
Slowly, strangling... my soul.
A malady that seeps,
from every, weary... pore.
A wen.
That's left its, bodily mark.
Felt, by only me,
and me

... alone!

414) Ó Dhubh Téigh Dhubh

Is breá dorrain d'fhág a scar ar dom.
Níl le blackness,
Líonann mo chorp.
Go mall, tachtadh... m'anam.
A sileadh malady,
dul síos, tuirseach... pore.
A bán.
An bhfuil d'fhág 'go' marc fisiciúil.
Más mian leat, ach le haghaidh dom,
agus i
... Aonair!

415) Pure Aleatoricism, Music To

More than just...
Mere, aeolian tones.
I whistle, a haunting,
Non-melodious tune,
That rambles in my head.
That's too sad...
for even words,
to know.
Though it's truly...
Sheer mellifluous
To

My ears...

416) And What Do They... Know

They say,
There's plenty more fish in sea.
Well, they should try and tell,
the Mangarahara that...
Albeit, I consider my heart, prehensile.
With those, whom, I love.
When all's said, and done.
I guess, I'm just an endemic, kinda guy.
However
I just don't want to end up,
like...
A Lonesome George!
In

Any way.

417) Her Colour Matched The

Luminescence, of her skin.
And the incandescence of her eyes.
Take me on down...
That lonesome, road.
A journey, unfinished...
Somewhere, along the way.
I went and lost you.
And though I stopped.
But... there you were.
Like a winter's wisp.
Gone... vanished.
Like a flock of snipes!
Before the dawn.
Under those bleak
Grey December

Skies.

418) I Have an Appetite Though

I'd forgotten...
Amidst the fear, the death, and...
the apathy.
The sweet smell... Of
Love... life...
The lingering, scent...
of... a woman.
The taste!
Moments,
that touch, the essence... of our souls.
I'd forgot, that sometimes.
We must, still... chase the dream.
And yet

I yearn for love!

419) Just Remember

Every, sunrise.
Is a dream...

Yet to happen.

420) My Life...

Once,
tears... were sweet,
brought... by joy.
Now they're bitter,
and they burn.
Though they flow, the same.
Elation, mixed with sorrow.
A melody, that... unbidden plays.
Is sleep like death?
Just

Prelude... to a dream?

421) I've not much understood life, nor love

I hope comprehending death, is easier.

422) Times like this... I know...

But I wish...
That, I still smoked.
That, I could speak with you again.
That, pigs... could even fly!
I've no one to meet.
I've, no need... to... sleep.
For it only, speeds the morrow...
Pour me another drink, but hold the ice.
Tempestuous... to the last, that's me.
Now, show me... your teeth, and I'll show you... a
smile.
I'm ever emotional, to the last.
Resonate, within, the warmth,
of my love.
When
You've kissed the Devil's... daughter, and her
laughter's,
rocked... the heavens.
Disturbing angels, while they slumber.
Savour, the moment, so... you can, treasure it,
Please.
Just don't offend, the King of Norway.
So, leave me now, for...
You know.
Even, for all my virtues,
I'm still, going... to Valhalla!
And we're all

Bound, for hell!

423) Solari, a Consolation

Vodka is my muse, my solace and my ruin, and
although it oft lies to me, it does so, in a kinda nice,
drunken... way.
So I'm putting all those memories of you, in a bottle,
and locking it a cupboard.
If may, sometime... in the future, that we might meet
again, I'll have, just, the bottle...
That

We could share...

424) When Loved Ones Are Few

Sometimes,
for no explicable... reason.
My emotions, overshadow, my... thoughts.
Wherein, a sweet memory, turns... to sorrow.
Not unlike, a shadow cast...
upon, the sun.
A mood, like a cloud, that's filled...
That empties, then... passes on.
The sunny times, are few... and are, long, in... coming.
I'm needing blue skies, where clouds...
Are few

And far between.

425) When Things Come To

Pass... it's
Not much, to ask... ?
Just to see, a friendly... smile.
To hear, another's... voice.
Lonely's, still... lonely.
A heavy heart, a wistful, sigh.
I had more freedom, when... in gaol.
For, love... had never touched.
My heart was empty, like the night.
When prison bars... blocked out,
the stars.
I was young, and...
Knew you

Naught.

426) I've Not Yet...

Joined the eulipotyphla.
But I may... well be, on my way.
For the crocidurinae, have,
called... upon me.
After all, are we not, truly cladistic, in all our shapes,
and forms?
Shape, shadow, shine... silhouette.
I knew how, to hide... well.
Could, the piercing screams
That die, deep within my throat,
Taste any sweeter
Now you've

Gone... ?

427) Moody, Misty, Sunsets... Who

Shared my life, and truly know...
I have had enough, sad, silent... reminders
So... I need naught, the music... too.
Melodies, like memories.
A constant... Of inexplicable moods,
that turn... to tears.
Of majik times, that I... now know.
We're not born, from moments... spent.
With, just... one... love.
But a mélange, of all!
Of those beauties, and some quite not!
That I...
Once

Knew... ?

428) Soft is Your Breath...

I love the shadows, where I can hide.
Where none, sees my face, nor hears... my pain.
Where, all men, are... equal... Where, all... can bare,
their... soul.
And weep... undisturbed.
I heard, the whisper, of wings...
The fluttering, of... feathers.
Like the cry, of, the mocking jay.
Which, is only heard, by wretches...
Who, then... silently echo,
its lonely... call.
To appreciate, the beauty, of nature,
It's best, to have someone
To...
Share it with, and

Kiss the dream.

429) So Silently I Died... As

Sometimes,
I wonder, of the monster, that lurks... within.
Perhaps...
If it had, just remained physical, and...
I never, fell in love?
I reached, beyond... my dreams.
And searched, within the stars.
Within, a cosseted... moon.
Now crippled beyond all hope.
I remember, a, whispered... kiss!
That only you, and I, once shared.
That I thought, had hinted... more.
Some of us, nurture, a dream.
While others, hide behind reality.
When you've kissed a dream,
Reality,
will always be... in the pale

I hunger for your kiss.

430) Sometimes We All...

Spend... time.
Searching, for a little happiness.
I'm looking for a new day
Wild tattoos, and loud music... to calm my ears.
False love...
How long, does a shadow, creep... ?
Before it, drowns out... the sun!
I know killing, I know death.
I once knew love...
For, I smiled, and it was... returned.
Goodnight sweet child.
I'm old...
and

must sleep...

431) My Perceptions Filled My Mind With

Sensations... for.
I've tasted, that rainbow.
I've, reached... for the stars!
I've cried, tears of blood.
Speak, no more of God.
For, he's cast me, down.
I may chase, a lost horizon!
But my dreams, remain...
Earthbound.
Who... would throw, a skipping... stone?
Or whisper, to... a horse?
Or ride a cloud, into a sunset?
Ask, no more... of me,
I've seen, through all the lies!
I've seen, wondrous times.
I've seen...
a meteorological phenomenon.
Smelling all...
Its

Colours...

432) *Some Things Are...*

Never said... so.
Tell them, one... day,
that... you
Knew me.
That,
You, knew me,
well...
Perhaps, we'd shared...
A brief interlude... in paradise or hell.
A trench, a drink, or perhaps... once. We'd shared... a
bed.
Or, it was with my words...
that'd you'd, once... read.
But not love.
That it seems
Was

Never shared.

433) In Quiet Moments, There's Times

Deep, deep, down...
Beyond, where I think, and I can see.
Where lies a memory,
that haunts, my tears.
And, every now, and when,
For some, unknown... reason
One, escapes my eye, and flows.
And sadness fills me.
For, I know... not
Why

I cry...

434) Just a Point...

Who, sees... my joy,
or hears, my... laugh,
within, these four walls?
Who, feels...
My hot tears,
as sorrow...
Runs, its course.
Turn your back,
and... feed me,
to the wolves!
Pain
is fused, within...
my bones.
For a heart's,
too... brittle,
and...
Oft

they break...

435) I Miss Your Voice, Your Words Still

Speak volumes.
For...
I'd kiss your feet
To taste, your lips... again.
I'd kill, to see, your... smile!
Don't ask...
About, hearing... of,
your laugh!
As... Armageddon
May

Resound.

436) A Tired Pen, With...

A broken feather...
I spend my waking hours
Searching for my dreams... and,
In trying, to... hold... back,
the night...
And everything,
it brings.
I've seen, every... kind of sunset, and I've shared,
more dawns
... than, you could, ever... know.
So...
Painted lady, tell me...
Are they emblems of your...
forgotten love?
Or are they lost moments, from
deep within, your past...
Why then, do you hide them...
'neath your clothes?
I know each one... For
I've kissed... each, and
every

Weary, ink!

437) Secrets Perished, While Fate Did

Deal his smoky cards, tinged
With, burning flame.
I cry, for things, I've... lost.
For things, and, the happiness
They brought, but I never, had.
A season's, chill...
The, weather's... change,
Has, brought me... pain.
Makes, my wounds... All,
burn again!
Staring down, that darkened... road.
I looked beyond... the saucer, and, its cup!
For fear, lay... beyond, the darkness.
Beyond... the searing tracer.
Where, bullets killed, or...
burned a track.
Through mortal flesh.
To, cripple... a mind.
To, scar... a soul.
I'll pick my tree, with care.
Perhaps, hidden... well from view.
Or on a ridge,
to see, one last... sunset.
And there I'll

carve my name.

438) While You Were...

Abed.
Was my touch, so light?
You did, dreamt...
of a spider, in the night.
Not, of my kiss.
My osculation,
whilst... you slept.
Though I smelled, your musk.
Of which, heavily... I drank.
I crept away
And left you

Sleeping.

439) Not,

fame... nor... fortune
Do I seek.
Love, is what I search for.
The elusiveness, of an emotion, that's beyond... mere,
riches.
Though for some the latter.
Is... ever
dogged

with tragedy.

440) Life's...

Snowflakes fell...
Like cotton... candy.
Landing on,
My... eyelashes.
If I spoke, within a dream
And told you that I loved you,
Would it be, or would it not?
A memory or
just

A dream?

For Amanda Ward because she asked.

441) Tears Fall Once

Whilst... I sit,
And dream.
As yet again
I search for...
That most...
Handsome man
In all the world!
To hold, to cherish.
To make love... To
Once

Again

For Cath Hartley because she asked.

442) Are We Not All, But a Few...

In a chosen minority
A young man, an old man.
A dead man, and a forgotten man.
A real man, a ladies' man, a man's man.
Man's inhumanity, towards man.
Man oh...
Man

Just... men?

For Mary Trundle because she asked.

443) Hey Beautiful, Don't

You know.
I saw a sad, and...
lonely beauty.
For in none, of your pictures,
do you smile.
I thought, that I, could... change that, for you.
At the moment.
You're "awesome"... enough,
for me.
For in your current mode
I've felt your sighs, and I've heard you cry.
Time now, for... happy tears, and picture smiles, once
more.
You've said... but...
I think there is, more chance... of You, breaking... my
heart, than Me, causing You,
further... pain.
Just to be, in the same place, with you, and hear you
laugh,
To see, the colour... of,
your eyes.
I'd gladly sit, and just hold your hand.
As my heart, would sigh...
a happy

sigh.

For Tone Lise Dahl because she asked.

444) Sing Me a Lullaby

So I can dream.
And
Know, I'll wake tomorrow.
I'll sleep safe, within
Your arms.
I'll feel the sweetness
Of your breath...
Upon, on my cheeks
That run wet,
With silent, tears.
Kiss me, as I sleep.
Soft

Like an angel would.

For Christine Meyers because she asked.

445) *Sad, But...*

What... could love... be?
Without, a bit of...
Muddied history,
Or, passion?
With us, baby girl
I truly doubt...
That it'd, ever be, a little bit... boring or dull!
I, can only say
Each and every day...
I love you...
And you know that... that
Is

True.

For Suzette Lee McCabe because she asked.

446) *Would you drive my car, Baby Girl?*

On the road to oblivion,

And still, only halfway...
To... paradise.
When, grey eyes, turn to blue.
I smelled beautiful...
And, the beautiful... was you.
Skin, as soft as... velvet.
Trembling, to the touch!
I long, to hold you, close.
I long, to taste, your lips.
To cleanse, your fears, and
kiss, your tears.
What I need
Is

A travelling companion.

For Faye Sparkes because she's a twin.

447) Until

Until you have had the ground beneath your feet
disappear.
Seen the sky turn black
and shower you with molten metal fragments.
You'll never know how precious the morning can be
for men at war.
I pray you never have to share the moment.

For Becky Jane Mellin, 20 years an army wife.

448) It's Only a Name

Somewhere out there,
A scribe has penned my name.
And added me...
to "The Book of Sighs".
In an unknown chapter,
Containing an unknown verse.
With only one line!
But the name it contains...

... is mine.

For Jimalene Carroll because she asked.

449) It's True

Dreams, are made... from
The colours, of the rainbow.
Which
Slowly, fall... to earth.
Like Majik dust, spread by fairies.
To, infest our hearts, briefly?
Then, they are gone!
When cloudy skies, and windswept plains... lay empty.
Washed away, by the rain.
Newly coloured flowers sway.
Skies are blue.
That rainbow's... gone.
As are, my lost dreams... now.
Nature's bouquet,
For

Romance.

For Michelle Lowther because she asked.

450) When Alcohol and Dreams Conspire

I hold a dream.
But, I'll not tell.
We, all have... Secrets!
Some, are... Wishes.
Though.
I'll never hold another.
Like, I once... held you.
There'll be no scent, that may assail.
I'll only ever, taste.
A forgotten dream...
Of what I had.
A
Tender
Moment... A tattoo
That was rebirth
And what

I see, is a forgotten memory of you!

451) Once But Not...

While a snowflake melts
Your answers... .
Are whispers in the wind.
Like rustling leaves.
Or that "noise"... just before,
The thunder breaks.
Or a pebble... as it sinks.
As ripples hit the shore!
All of this I've heard.
But it doesn't matter

Anymore.

452) Can Yea Hear...

While you're all alone...
the thunder...
when it, rolls... !
Down, the valley.
When it lets the Afanc, swim, and cross the lake.
All the while... lightning, splits... the night.
And as...
Ceffyl Dwr, rides its frothy waves,
The Cwn Annwn is loose, and... is... hunting!
Your man, is gone...
So you clutch your pillow, and
You hide...

from Cyhraeth's knock.

453) Will We Meet... In The

Twilight... beckons, to... romance.
While candles, flicker.
As trysts are begun, so...
Lovers... play, their games.
Where pain,
has met... passion
Dark secrets,
are oft, laid... bare.
With a ragged, fingernail.
He etched,
a heart, upon...
her trembling

flesh.

454) Speak My Name for I'm

In my cups.
Would, that I,
Upon a drunken, dream,
Didst meet, my... true love.
And, as such she was perfection.
And would remain... intact.
I'm sad, but I'm glad.
Cause, I'm... missing you.
And though, we've never... met!
I've kissed you, every... night.
Though I always...
woke

Alone.

455) Today's The

Last time that... I'll...
Ice cold pillows, that melt.
Like a lover's heart, within my arms.
Soft down, to soothe the pain.
Darkness, that holds no rest.
But keeps sleep... at bay!
How soon till dawn?
The start
of another, lonely

Day.

456) Love's Mirrored In

The Shhhhh...
No names now.
Put your head, upon my chest.
So I can hold you, tight!
And, shield you from,
the... demons, of the night.
Sigh, a little sigh, of...
Sheer contentment.
As, I hold your hand, in your sleep.
Smile, your wistful smile.
For when you awake.
I'll see, that spark, of... desire.
Of a promise...
In those, baby blue,
Baby, girl's

Eyes.

457) I'll Remember

As...
Dead leaves, rustle... !
On empty streets.
While the wind,
steals away, your name...
from, my whispering lips.
I've broken a promise!
And now, must pay.
My heart is dull, and heavy.
Love's spark... Well.
Who knows I miss you more each moment.
I'll miss, always
until

That first kiss.

458) I've Seen You...

And I know,
Not all, Angels...
are made of, nor are, etched... in stone.
Not all, angels... live in heaven.
There's them, down here, that, live... alone.
They wait, they watch, they...
Walk, among us.
While you sleep.
They soothe... your brow allay your fears.
They... steal, your pain.
... Dry, your tears.
But, it burns, them... out.
That's why, the world's.
Full... of chaos.
There's, not... enough,
Angels... To...
Go

Round.

For Donna Louise Armstrong because she said it was
her favourite.

459) Objective Reality...

Not, for peace of mind, of... late.
Merely, come habitude.
And the coin,
that lays, within... my pocket!
It, brings... no cheer, or respite.
Only smiles, from... the barkeep.
Chilled beers...
And a ticket, to... oblivion.
Still yet, I struggle with my sleep.
A lost sense of purpose?
Though it's only in my dreams, I seek.
No consolation.
No
Solace... do I find.

460) Tell Me,

Have you ever felt true poena?
Or
A tiredness, beyond... belief.
For only them, that's been.
Truly knows...
And
I'm hoping one day,
With all that's between me, and
the coming, of the dawn.
I'll lose this melancholy!
For
I'm hiding behind...
a single blade, of bison grass.
Now, that you, have... gone.
For you were so beautiful
It hurt my eyes, to watch you... and.
After all
Who wants to die... alone?

461) Being Intimate

It's dark,
and, secluded!
It's terribly chic!
Its suave... and, debonair.
It's dinner.
It's a table, for two!
And I'm sharing it.
With... an empty chair.
If I promised to take you to the moon...
Would, you let me...
take you

on the floor?

462) Don't Judge Me

Because of the silence.
For I can still hear them.
They call me, by name.
And, I can, still... see them.
When, no one's there.
They've come to claim me.
But, they're too late.
For
I'm long past, being... just tired.
And my flesh, bears the scars.
Mourn me, for... who, I was.
Not, who I became.
And while I'm dead
I'll party, in my head.
Until the dream... is,
no more.
Because

You never knew who I was...

463) I'm Lethargic I'm Tired

I'm just, so... tired.
Would be, that... when
I dribbled, in my sleep!
That, a memory, that... lingered
Caused, my...
Thoughts, to wander?
Could I wish, for something
I never, ever, really... had?
Or
For someone, I never,
really... never,
knew?
Could a memory, of... another.
Bring solace?
Or a haunting loss?
Didst, I wrest,
the passion, from... my dreams?
In order, to quell, dark thoughts?
Or, has lost love...
Tainted, all
That I think...
or
that I see?

I feel, I'm dying... inside.

464) I Drink

To blur, the visions.
To stop, the colour... in my dreams.
To pause, the video that plays, within
my head.
So all I see...
... is darkness

While my life is on pause...

About the Author

James Love, AKA Jock, the bear of a man and one I'm proud to call a friend.

Jim was born in Glasgow on 31st March 1955. He went to schools in both Canada and in Scotland. After a brief spell in the City of Glasgow Police, he joined the Army in 1973. February 1974 he volunteered for parachute training.

Upon graduating P Company and on completion of his jump training, Jim joined 'I' Parachute Battery, Bull's Troop, 7th Parachute Regiment Royal Horse Artillery. He joined the Black Knights Freefall Team as a junior member and won the Army Novice Accuracy Championship in 1977. In 1977 as part of the defence cuts the regiment lost its airborne role and was posted to Osnabruck in Germany. Jim disappeared whilst in Germany and joined the French Foreign Legion...

There he made the rank of Corporal and was an instructor in the depot of R.I.L.E. in Castelnaudary. Unfortunately, the pay and conditions were not the greatest and Jim decided to "leave" and re-join the British Army. After getting out of France, he hitchhiked back to Osnabruck in West Germany where his unit was then stationed – walking the last 80 kilometres in a blizzard. After being tried by Court-Martial (under Section 38 of the Army Act 1955), Jim served 7 months and 11 days of his subsequent sentence (6 weeks of it in solitary) having earned 3 months and 4 days' remission of sentence for good behaviour.

He returned to Aldershot and joined the Parachute contingent of 4th Field Regiment Royal Artillery. There he was part of the Pre-Parachute selection staff and in his time helped train a few officers who subsequently reached the ranks of Colonel, Brigadier and even one who made it to Major General.

Whilst not training prospective paratroopers. He was part of a small team that worked directly with the parachute infantry soldier and was attached initially to B Company of the 2nd Battalion the Parachute Regiment as a member of the Forward Observation Party (as a signaller for the officer directing artillery fire) On the run-up to the cruise south in 1982, Jim was given 4 hours off to get married on the 20th of April. Two days before reaching the islands Jim was told that he couldn't go ashore as he had "signed off". As a consequence, Jim had to re-enlist. After going ashore with the first wave on the 21st of May, Jim was then transferred to A Company whilst on top of Sussex Mountains in the Falkland Islands due to another member of an OP crew falling foul of the OC of the Company. Jim served on attachment to A Coy until June 1982 when the unit returned to the Battery (29 Corunna 4th Field Regiment, Royal Artillery) and 2 Para sailed home to the UK on the "Norland". The unit flew out some weeks later but only got as far as being assigned to guard Argentine General Menendez and the other Argentinean prisoners on the "St Edmund" ferry. So, he became 'Class of 82'.

Having bought himself out of the Army in 1991 for £200, Jim is now employed by the Ministry of Defence Guard Service at Tedworth House in Wiltshire as part of the MOD security team for the PRAC and H4H. Previously he was employed as

Group Manager at various establishments on Salisbury Plain controlling the unarmed guarding capabilities at DSTL Porton Down and DBRNC Winterbourne Gunner but to name two, and responsible for establishing the only "Overt" MOD PAT Dog sections in the UK.

During his time in the armed forces Jim completed 4 tours of Northern Ireland, served in the war of '82, and gained many qualifications, which unfortunately are solely militarily orientated. He has however gained a multitude of brothers from other mothers. Jim is single and lives in Tidworth.

When not working or in a quiet moment Jim writes the odd line of poetry, of which some has been translated from English to Spanish, Turkish, Scots Gaelic and Welch Gaelic and has been included in several compilations of poetry. He has recently completed a Mental Health First Aid at work course, and enjoys the rapport of the Veterans and Wounded Injured Soldiers who attend Tedworth House. A former Paratrooper but Forever Airborne.

Some of his medals and achievements include the GSM NI, SAM with Rosette, British Wings, American Wings, Canadian Wings, Basic Military Parachutist, Military Freefall Parachutist, Sniper, Combat Survival Instructor, ADV Op Ack (had the role and function of the Forward Observation Officer due to being a captain short in the regiment) AFV Instructor, Advanced Signaller (RSI), Small Arms Instructor...

We thank you for your service, Jim.

Jay Morgan Hyrons, 2020

Jay Morgan Hyrons is herself an accomplished author. Her latest book is on release now entitled: 'And She Danced', the first of a powerful and deeply moving trilogy. Written as a Biographical Fiction, it is based on the extraordinary life of Jay Morgan Hyrons. The book is dedicated to her late husband LCpl Gary Bingley MM & the Parachute Regiment.

https://www.amazon.co.uk And She Danced
https://www.jaymorganhyrons.com
https://falklands35blog.wordpress.com

Remember...
Our tomorrow is their future.

My son Callum James Love
02/10/1999

Printed in Great Britain
by Amazon